The Source for Nonverbal Learning Disorders

Sue Thompson

Skill Area:	Nonverbal Learning Disorders
Age Level:	All ages

LinguiSystems

LinguiSystems, Inc.
3100 4th Avenue
East Moline, IL 61244-9700

1-800-PRO IDEA
1-800-776-4332

FAX: 1-800-577-4555
E-mail: service@linguisystems.com
Web: www.linguisystems.com

TDD: 1-800-933-8331
(for those with hearing impairments)

About the Author

Sue Thompson, M.A., C.E.T., is an Educational Consultant and Therapist. She specializes in training educators and educational therapists to understand and provide appropriate interventions for individuals with NLD. Sue taught for over 20 years in California Public Schools in both regular and special education classrooms. She holds a Master's Degree in Special Education from St. Mary's College of California. Sue has written numerous articles on learning and behavior and writes a regular column for the *GRAM* (A publication of LDA-CA). She provides teacher inservice training, workshops, and presentations for professionals and parent groups.

The Source for Nonverbal Learning Disorders is Sue's first publication with LinguiSystems.

October, 1997

Dedication

To Nicholas

Table of Contents

Foreword

"Sue Thompson's [book] is an important and valuable work that demystifies the nature and needs of the child with Nonverbal Learning Disabilities. This child presents a puzzling and challenging profile to teachers and parents. Much scholarly research has been completed related to NLD. However, Thompson's great contribution is the translation of this research into an understandable manual for the identification and treatment of these children and youths.

"This book is filled with useful checklists, anecdotes, methods, and resources. [It is] a valuable addition to any professional bookshelf. Armed with this manual, a professional or parent can make a meaningful difference in the development and education of the child with NLD."

Richard D. Lavoie
Executive Director, Riverview School
Producer, *How Difficult Can This Be? The F.A.T. City Workshop*

I had been working in various special education programs in California for nearly 15 years in 1985, had specialist credentials in the areas of learning and behavior, had received my master's degree in Special Education, and had never heard of *nonverbal learning disabilities syndrome*. Then I received a transfer student from a New Jersey school district with an IEP specifying the condition of NLD. Twelve years later, I have pored over extensive literature and research and have personally worked with hundreds of children and adults with NLD.

During my inservice presentations to parents and teachers on the topic of NLD over the past seven years, participants have constantly urged me to "write it down" — to collect all my information in a book form. So I did. The resulting manual, *I Shouldn't Have to Tell You!*, was self-published for almost a year, with an overwhelming outpouring of gratitude from my readers. The success of the self-published version prompted me to look for wider distribution, and the result is *The Source for Nonverbal Learning Disorders* a re-formatted version of my original book.

This manual grew out of pleas from both parents and professionals to have this information written in an easy-to-read, accessible format. I recently received an e-mail from a mom who wanted me to know that six of the professionals attending her daughter's IEP meeting had read my book. My suggestions for CAMS were used in developing her daughter's IEP. I now hear this type of heartwarming testimonial daily. Please use this book as a resource. The summaries, lists, and charts are provided for quick reference.

I hope this book will help inform and instruct both parents and educators about this under-recognized and poorly understood syndrome. It is my sincere wish that the strategies presented in this book will aid you in designing successful interventions for individuals with NLD, and thereby improve the quality of their lives. Working together we *can* make a difference. To quote a very special colleague of mine, Judy Lewis of Carmel, California, "This book will actually save lives."

Sue

Author's note: All of the examples described in this book arise from actual cases. They depict my personal experiences with children and adults exhibiting the characteristics of nonverbal learning disorders, which may or may not represent a typical sample. The names and certain distinguishing features of the clients have been changed to protect their privacy. Some examples are composites. My thanks are extended to the parents and individuals who permitted their stories to be told in the spirit of helping others. Their dilemmas, their quandaries, and their insights have been more instructive than any text to me. The children and adults I have assessed and worked with are my most valuable teachers!

Since both sexes are thought to be equally affected by the nonverbal learning disabilities syndrome, masculine and feminine terms are alternated equally throughout the book when referring to individuals with NLD, except when referring to specific individuals.

For the convenience of the reader, certain basic educational and neuropsychological terms used thoughout this book are defined in the **Glossary**, beginning on page 171.

Chapter 1

Introduction

Both parents and teachers will often suspect that something is amiss early on, but they can't quite put a finger on it . . .

Damon, an adorable pre-schooler with wispy blond hair and big blue eyes, turns four years old today. His grandparents take him out for a special birthday breakfast and then to look around at the local mall, while his parents and his older brother decorate their house for a surprise birthday party. It is no surprise to his parents that the grandparents are late in returning; this isn't the first time Damon "got lost" in a department store and mall security had to be enlisted to help locate him.

When the birthday boy finally arrives home, he immediately turns around to walk out again, saying, "Oops! This isn't my house!" The furniture has been rearranged in the front room, colorful streamers hang from the ceiling, and the entry hall is trimmed with balloons and cut-outs of his favorite cartoon characters. He isn't pretending or being silly; Damon truly doesn't recognize his own home.

Then, before Damon has a chance to exit, five of his little friends jump out from behind the couch and squeal "Surprise!" with obvious delight and uncontrollable laughter. Damon looks around and screams, too. But his is a scream of terror. He runs to his bedroom, stumbling several times along the way, dives under his bed, and steadfastly refuses to come out. His party continues without him, as various members of his family take turns trying to coax Damon out to join the celebrating. He does want to talk but he won't budge from his refuge — not even to open his presents.

What's Happening Here?

Damon's parents, who have worked hard to make this a perfect day for him, are perplexed. They begin to ask themselves familiar questions:

- Why is Damon always so opposed to anything novel — so attached to sameness?
- How can we help him grow out of his fears and allow him to enjoy life's surprises?

Even Damon's preschool teacher has expressed concerns about his "lack of adaptability." Damon's parents have many questions about their second son, who seems so different from their first son and from the other children his age. Their frustrations continue as they wonder:

- Why does Damon ask so many questions instead of exploring things on his own, the way other children do?

• Why does Damon always seem so ill at ease and awkward in social situations? It's as though he's unable to "look and learn."

Damon's parents are certain he's bright. He talked in phrases and sentences at fifteen months. He read road signs and cereal boxes by the time he was two years old, and now, at age four, Damon has a vocabulary to rival most adults. A learning disability is the last thing on their minds as they ruminate over the inconsistencies in Damon's development.

Damon's apparent precociousness in verbal skills has helped allay their concerns over some of his difficulties, which include the following:

• extreme clumsiness

• failure to recognize faces which should be familiar to him

• a poor sense of direction

• an aversion to anything novel

His parents feel certain Damon will do well in school because of his strengths in academic pursuits. They also feel confident he will outgrow his other idiosyncratic propensities.

Verbal
(35%)

Nonverbal
(65%)

Everyday Communication
Components

The Communication Link

There is no question that most scholastic accomplishments in our society are measured and defined through language-based communication. Yet, more than 65% of all communication is conveyed nonverbally. We're all familiar with nonverbal communication, but few professionals have been specifically trained to look for deficits in this area. And, although intelligence measures are designed to evaluate both the verbal and nonverbal aspects of intelligence, many educators tend to ignore evidence of nonverbal deficiencies in their students. Or worse, they brand students with nonverbal learning disabilities as "problem" children.

Everyone is aware of the important role language plays in human learning. The competence of an individual, as judged by our present-day society, is often linked to his verbal proficiencies. A person who speaks eloquently and has a well-developed vocabulary tends to be accorded more credibility than an individual who makes constant grammatical errors and demonstrates a limited vocabulary.

A student who has innate difficulties reading, spelling, or expressing himself stands out in most classroom

DEFINITION

nonverbal communication
Any communication that doesn't express language directly, but often augments it, including, facial expressions, gestures, body posture, and speaking distance.

situations. Likewise, a student who is a top reader, achieves excellent spelling scores, and expresses himself articulately usually *does not prompt his teacher to consider a learning disorder*. The student with nonverbal learning disabilities syndrome (NLD), however, is usually an excellent reader, a good speller, and an exceptional verbal communicator. The following are a few characteristics of NLD which might be observed prior to academic difficulties:

- The child talks incessantly.
- The child appears to ignore his teacher's disapproving facial expressions.
- The child is clumsy or uncoordinated for no apparent reason.
- The child has difficulty with visual-spatial-organizational tasks.
- The child makes inappropriate social remarks.
- The child has difficulty relating to his peers in an age-appropriate manner.

A more complete list of distinctive features can be found on page 15 — **Common Characteristics of Nonverbal Learning Disorders**.

Academic Development

Damon's father is a surgeon and his mother a social worker — both highly intelligent and highly educated professionals. They have read many books on child development and child-rearing. But neither of them had ever heard of *nonverbal learning disorders* when Damon turned four.

Later, when Damon began experiencing problems in school, his father was quick to attribute Damon's difficulties to his mother's "over-protective" tendencies. "If you didn't baby Damon so much, he'd be no different from the other kids," he'd berate his wife. Damon's mother was at a loss to explain why she felt Damon needed more defending and vigilance than their elder son had at the same age, but she somehow knew instinctively that he did. Damon seemed naive, trusting, and totally lacking in "street smarts."

The distinctions which set Damon apart from his peers continued to escalate throughout his early childhood, but his initial grades in school were excellent, owing to his exceptional rote memory, his strong verbal skills, and an almost fanatical sense of determination.

Damon did experience trouble with handwriting and mathematics, but merely worked harder than the other children to overcome these hinderances. Watching his early attempts at writing was painful. He had great difficulty copying material from the chalkboard and lining up the columns on his math papers. Damon never seemed to finish school assignments in the time allowed, so he put in additional time to complete the expected tasks. He missed recesses at school and had to drop out of after-school activities in order to try to keep up with his classmates.

When he reached fourth grade, where most of his schoolwork involved written responses, Damon began resisting any type of written work. By the time he entered fifth grade, a tremendous amount of friction had built up between Damon and his parents and teachers over his failure to complete assignments. His parents sought help from the school's Student Study Team, but received only empty encouragement:

- "He's a bright child who doesn't apply himself."
- "He'll be fine once he learns to better organize himself."

These explanations didn't match the picture of the Damon his parents saw. Eventually, they went outside the school and began what seemed to be an endless odyssey, dragging Damon from specialist to specialist, trying to fit together the pieces of the puzzle:

- A psychologist confirmed that their son was gifted.
- An occupational therapist confirmed his coordination difficulties.
- Many labels were tossed out, but no practical guidance was given to Damon's parents.

It wasn't until Damon turned 14 and was being treated for a *major depressive episode* that an insightful child psychologist finally diagnosed his nonverbal learning disorder, based upon this combination of factors:

- his early developmental history
- his present symptomology
- a significant discrepancy between his verbal IQ and his performance IQ

Damon's narrative isn't unusual for a child with nonverbal learning disabilities. It parallels that of many other children suffering from this under-recognized syndrome. The remainder of this Introduction focuses on defining the syndrome of nonverbal learning disabilities and providing some general information about its identification and need for early intervention.

NLD Explained

The discovery of the NLD syndrome began in the early 1970s, with research involving groups of learning-disabled children identified by discrepancies between their verbal and performance IQ scores. It is unfortunate that 25 years later, even professionals in the field of education are largely uninformed about or unfamiliar with nonverbal learning disorders, as these disabilities can be much more devastating to a child than language-based learning disorders (such as dyslexia), in the long run.

 The Source for Nonverbal Learning Disorders

right hemisphere
the area of the brain which processes nonverbal or performance-based information, including the visual-spatial, intuitive, organizational, evaluative, and holistic processing functions of an individual.

Since diminished access to or disordered functioning of the right-hemisphere systems *impedes all understanding and adaptive learning*, it is fair to say (as Helmer R. Myklebust did in 1975) that nonverbal learning disabilities "are more debilitating than verbal disabilities." The specific central processing abilities and deficits that characterize this syndrome are now well defined. Still, nonverbal learning disorders remain predominantly misunderstood and largely go unrecognized. Current evidence and theories suggest destruction, disorder, or dysfunction of white matter (long, myelinated fibers in the brain) in the right hemisphere could be the cause for nonverbal learning disorders. Researchers have observed symptomology similar to that found in inviduals with NLD in patients with known neurological insults such as the following:

- moderate to severe head injury
- repeated radiation treatments
- congenital absence of the corpus callosum
- treatment for hydrocephalus
- removal of brain tissue from the right hemisphere

corpus callosum
wide band of neural fibers connecting the two cerebral hemispheres

All of these neurological insults involve a significant destruction of white matter connections in the right hemisphere, which are important for intermodal integration.

A child's earliest mode of communication should be nonverbal. As we have seen in the case of Damon, both parents and teachers will often suspect that something is amiss early on, but they can't quite put a finger on it. Three categories of dysfunction will present themselves:

- **motoric** — a lack of coordination, severe balance problems, difficulties with fine graphomotor skills
- **visual-spatial-organizational** — a lack of image, poor visual recall, faulty spatial perceptions, difficulties with spatial relations
- **social** — a lack of ability to comprehend nonverbal communication, difficulties adjusting to transitions and novel situations, significant deficits in social judgment and social interaction.

Early consultation with a school psychologist or family physician typically only serves to dismiss or minimize a teacher's or parent's worries about this child. More often than not, parents are assured that everything is fine and their child's behavior is written off as one of these:

- perfectionistic and/or obsessive/compulsive
- immature
- the result of boredom with the way things are normally done
- mere clumsiness

Until recently, a parent's or teacher's concerns were rarely given any credence unless the child reached a point in school where he was no longer able to function, given the limitations of this neurological syndrome or, in some cases, the child suffered a nervous breakdown, or worse.

A Closer Look at NLD Dysfunctions

Motoric

The child with nonverbal learning disorders commonly appears awkward and is, in fact, inadequately coordinated in both fine and gross-motor skills. He may have had extreme difficulty learning to ride a bike or kick a soccer ball. Fine-motor skills, such as cutting with scissors or tying shoelaces, seem impossible for this child to master. He talks his way through even simple motor activities. A young child with NLD is less likely to explore his environment motorically because he can't rely upon kinesthetic processing and spatial perceptions.

Visual-Spatial-Organizational

In the early years, a child such as Damon may appear confused much of the time (he *is* confused) despite a high intelligence and high scores on receptive and expressive language measures. The blank stares of this child come from failing to comprehend the interactions going on around him. However, this same blank stare is often misinterpreted by adults as manipulative behavior. Because this child does not give off any nonverbal cues as to how he's feeling or what he's thinking, parents and teachers may assume he's hiding something. Nothing could be further from the truth.

Owing to visual-spatial disturbances, it is difficult for this child to change from one activity to another or to move from one place to another. A child with NLD uses all of his concentration and attention to merely get through a room. Imagine the child's frustration when he attempts to function in a complicated or new social situation (such as Damon experienced at his surprise birthday party). Owing to his inability to handle such informational processing demands, the child with NLD will instinctively avoid any kind of novelty.

Social

A closer observation of the child will reveal a social ineptness brought about by misinterpretations of body language and/or tone of voice. Damon's parents were correct in noting that their child didn't seem to "look and learn." A child with NLD is unable to perceive subtle cues in his environment such as the ones listed on the next page.

12 *The Source for Nonverbal Learning Disorders*

- when something has gone "far enough"
- the idea of "personal space"
- facial expressions of others
- nonverbal signals that another person is registering pleasure (or displeasure)

All of the above are social skills that are normally grasped intuitively through observation, not directly taught. If a child is constantly being admonished with the words "I shouldn't have to tell you this!" it should alert everyone that something is awry, because *you do have to tell him everything*. The child's verbal processing may be very proficient, but it can still be impossible for him to receive and comprehend nonverbal information. Such a child will cope by relying upon language as his principal means of social relating, information gathering, and relief from anxiety. As a result, he is constantly being told, "You talk too much!"

Do You Know This Child?

The child with NLD will develop an exceptional memory for rote material, a coping skill he has had to hone in order to survive. Since the nonverbal processing area of his brain isn't giving him the needed automatic feedback, he relies solely upon his memory of past experiences, each of which he has labeled verbally, to guide him in future situations. This child learns little from experience or repetition and is unable to generalize information, so he doesn't apply past learning to new situations. His rigid reactions are less effective and less reliable than those of someone who is able to sense and interpret another person's social cues spontaneously (because of the vast array of differences in human nature).

Cumbersome monologues are another trait of a child with nonverbal learning disabilities. Normal conversational give-and-take seem to elude him. Teachers complain of a child who "talks incessantly" and parents complain, "He just doesn't seem to know when to be quiet!"

The Importance of Intervention

The urgency of identifying and servicing children with nonverbal learning disorders is especially acute. Overestimates of the child's abilities and unrealistic demands made by parents and teachers can lead to ongoing emotional problems for the child, who often develops generalized feelings of hopelessness and helplessness resulting from the unreliable perceptions and inaccurate interpretations which affect his judgments about the world around him and his interactions with other people. He will most likely receive a disproportionate share of criticism, reprimands, punishment, teasing, ostracism, and scapegoating. A favorable prognosis for this child seems to depend upon *early identification and intervention*. The child with NLD is particularly inclined towards seriously debilitating forms of internalizing psychopathology including:

- depression
- withdrawal
- panic attacks
- anxiety
- suicide (in some cases)

Pediatric neurospychologist Dr. Byron P. Rourke of the University of Windsor and his associates have found that nonverbal learning disabilities "predispose those afflicted to adolescent and adult depression and suicide risk." The child with NLD is regularly punished and picked-on for circumstances he can't help, without ever really understanding why, and he is, in turn, often left with little hope that his situation will ever improve. After amassing years of embarrassing and misconceived unintentional social blunders, it's not too difficult to understand how a person with nonverbal learning disorders could come to the conclusion that he does not fit in.

14 *The Source for Nonverbal Learning Disorders*

Common Characteristics of Nonverbal Learning Disorders

- ❑ performance IQ significantly lower than verbal IQ

- ❑ early speech and vocabulary development

- ❑ remarkable rote memory skills

- ❑ attention to detail

- ❑ early reading skills development, excellent spelling skills

- ❑ expresses himself eloquently

- ❑ lack of coordination

- ❑ severe balance problems

- ❑ difficulties with fine motor skills

- ❑ lack of image, poor visual recall

- ❑ faulty spatial perceptions

- ❑ difficulties with spatial relations

- ❑ lack of ability to comprehend nonverbal communication

- ❑ difficulties adjusting to transitions and new situations

- ❑ significant deficits in social judgment and interaction

Chapter 2
Identifying the Child With Nonverbal Learning Disorders

Many of the early symptoms of nonverbal learning disabilities instill pride, rather than alarm, in parents and teachers . . .

Keisha, an attractive African American girl with intense brown eyes and thick black braids, is the older of two almost identical looking girls born eleven months apart. When they were babies, their parents thought the two sisters would be very close and do everything together. But it seemed from the beginning that their styles of interacting were quite different, as was their approach to the world. Younger sister Shana was always into everything, while Keisha remained content to sit back and ask questions. Keisha wanted to know the name for everything and rapidly built her vocabulary, while Shana still wasn't talking at age five. Keisha thrilled her parents when she taught herself to read at age three. Shana couldn't even recite the alphabet when she entered first grade, after two years of speech and educational therapy.

The girls' parents, who are both well-educated (father is an attorney and mother a paralegal), determined early on that Shana was going to need some special support to make it through school. As a toddler, Shana's needs were identified by her local school district, and she began a weekly speech therapy program. She was placed in a special at-risk pre-kindergarten program providing daily educational therapy for her at age four. Keisha, on the other hand, was thought to be quite capable of progressing well without any interventions. She was placed in an accelerated program for gifted students when she entered school because she was already reading at a fifth-grade level.

Keisha was considered an excellent reader because she could read the words in books far beyond her grade level. But, although she remembered numerous specific details about what she had read, she was never able to figure out the main idea or the theme of even a first-grade story. Her parents and teachers showed little concern over her minor difficulties, which included:

- continually falling out of her chair
- an inability to hold her pencil correctly
- frequently getting lost on the school grounds
- talking incessantly
- making "inappropriate" comments to adult authority figures

If anything, at age six, Keisha was considered spoiled and perhaps a bit of a show-off. In short, the problems she was experiencing were written off as behavioral in nature.

Warning Signs are Welcome at First

Language-based disabilities are usually readily apparent to parents and educators early on. Nonverbal learning disorders, however, routinely go unrecognized. Many of the early symptoms of nonverbal learning disabilities instill pride, rather than alarm, in parents and teachers who ordinarily applaud language-based accomplishments. Some of these early signs might include these:

- a child considered gifted in early childhood by parents and teachers.
- an extremely verbose child who "speaks like an adult" at two or three years of age.
- a preschooler who reads by rote at a very young age (as was the case with Keisha)
- an eager, enthusiastic learner who quickly memorizes rote material, only serving to reinforce the notion of her precocity

Extraordinary early speech and vocabulary development aren't often suspected to be coping strategies used by a child who has a very deficient right-hemisphere system and limited access to her nonverbal processing abilities. The child with NLD is also likely to acquire an unusual aptitude for producing "phonetically accurate" reproductions of words (spelling), but few adults will consider this to be a reflection of her overdependence upon auditory perceptions (as opposed to visual or tactile). Likewise, remarkable rote memory skills, attention to detail, and a natural facility for decoding, encoding, and early reading development, do not generally cause red flags to go up. Yet, these are some of the important early indicators that a child, such as Keisha, is having difficulty relating to, and functioning in, her world nonverbally, and a warning that she has developed an excessive reliance upon her verbal skills.

Although this child hears the language being spoken around her, she may have difficulty understanding it. Figurative speech, idioms, sarcasm, and any nonliteral language patterns are like a foreign language to her. Imagine the confusion you would experience if the people around you suddenly began speaking in a language that you didn't know. This experience would become even more frustrating if you thought you recognized some of their words, but the words didn't seem to mean what you thought they meant. You would probably feel very uncomfortable, wondering why they were laughing at you or pointing at you. What did you do wrong? Why can't you understand them? This type of bewilderment is felt by the child with NLD throughout the day, every day of her life.

A Child Grows Into NLD

Keisha did fairly well in school until she reached fifth grade. At that time, her parents began participating in countless meetings regarding both academic and "behavioral" concerns expressed by her school staff. A few sessions of family counseling led to the suggestion that Keisha's problems in school were deliberate, possibly due to her jealousy over the extra attention extended to her younger sister Shana.

At first, this revelation caused her parents to feel guilty. *Could Keisha's strange behavior and other school problems actually be the result of their own lack of attention towards her?* Then they began to bristle, because they had worked very hard to achieve their present status in life, and they now saw their gifted daughter throwing away her potential by "intentionally misbehaving" at school. They wondered why she did not take advantage of all the wonderful opportunities they had given her. They punished Keisha when calls and notes about her "behavior" came home from her school and they placed considerable pressure on her to shape up. Instead, Keisha shut down.

School assignments were only half-completed and rarely handed in for credit. Keisha would sit at her desk in school and stare at a piece of paper for 15 or 20 minutes, unable to get her thoughts onto the paper. She became a frequent visitor to the school principal for:

- *tardiness* (getting lost on campus)
- *defiant behavior* (not completing assignments)
- *disruptiveness* (knocking over objects, falling out of her seat, talking out of turn)
- *general rudeness and lack of respect* (talking back to adults, using an inappropriate tone of voice).

By sixth grade, Keisha's grades had dropped from A's and B's to D's and F's. She began to see herself as a "bad person" and became discouraged and depressed. A referral for special education assessment was made at school, which resulted in the recommendation that Keisha be placed in a Special Day Class for severely emotionally disturbed students. After a visit to the class, her parents didn't agree to the placement because they knew Keisha's problems were different from the other students they saw there. Although this intervention solution didn't meet Keisha's needs, her parents feared her situation at school had gotten out of control. Recognizing that their punishments (no matter how severe) didn't alter Keisha's behavior, they eventually placed her in a diagnostic/treatment center at age 12. A thorough neuropsychological evaluation confirmed that Keisha met the diagnostic criteria for NLD.

Dr. Byron P. Rourke and his associates have found that the dysfunctions associated with NLD are "less apparent at the age of 7 to 8 years . . .

than at 10 to 14 years," and that they become "progressively more apparent (and more debilitating) as adulthood approaches." The **Developmental Profile of NLD Through the Lifespan** on pages 22-25 illustrates the progression of problems a child with NLD might face over the years.

Although a child may have a history of poor coordination and was probably slow to acquire motor skills, initial academic concerns about this child will typically come from the fact that she is not completing and/or turning in written assignments during her late elementary school years. She produces limited written output and the process is always slow and laborious for her.

When the skills for organizing and developing written work don't advance at the expected rate for a student, finally, the red flags go up. However, by this time, the child with NLD may have already "shut down" (like Keisha), or become firmly locked into an oppositional struggle with the adults in his life (like Damon in Chapter 1). These avoidance and confrontational approaches are coping mechanisms to deal with the academic pressures and performance demands which have been placed upon the student with NLD by unsuspecting parents and teachers, which this child is unable to meet.

The Consequences of Not Recognizing NLD

Serious repercussions may result if a child's nonverbal learning disorders are not recognized early and appropriately accommodated. It is clear that a child with NLD will not develop to her true potential without intensive intervention throughout her schooling. She will have difficulty making and keeping friends, unless social cues are defined and pointed out to her. She will miss out on important learning at school and her grades will plummet, unless her visual-spatial-organizational problems and dysgraphia are addressed and accommodated.

Adults may begin telling her that she is lazy and she will believe them, even though she is working ten times harder than her peers to accomplish much less. This form of negative commentary from teachers, friends, and family will cause this child to see herself in a predominantly negative light, and these negative feelings can spiral into full-blown depression. A child thus treated will subsequently cease to experience any fun in her existence. By adolescence, she may withdraw and refuse to take part in any social activities. And, as she sees her situation becoming more and more hopeless, feeling that no one out there understands her, at the most tragic extreme, her sense of hopelessness may culminate in teen suicide.

More than 5,000 teenagers in the United States commit suicide annually. Byron P. Rourke reports that children with NLD exhibit a higher incidence of suicidal behavior in adolescence than the norm. Therefore, it is absolutely imperative that interventive steps be taken by the family and the school staff working with the child burdened with NLD, to lessen the likelihood of this shattering consequence resulting from this disability.

Parents are in the best position to observe their child close at hand on a daily basis and to become staunch advocates for this child. No one knows the child better or loves her more than her parents. Pediatricians, teachers, and other professionals *must* take the time to listen carefully to the concerns reported by parents that may indicate the presence of non-verbal learning disabilities. Professionals in the field of special education must hone their diagnostic skills, in order to identify and provide services for students with NLD at an earlier age, before the plunging spiral of negativity erodes their feelings of self-worth.

Developmental Profile of NLD Through the Lifespan

There is no single, uniform presenting picture of a child with nonverbal learning disorders. However, a homogeneous cluster of signposts, manifesting within a framework of developmental stages can often be observed as illustrated by the following profile.

Infant and Toddler Years (0-2)

1. does not explore the world motorically

2. speech and language develop early

3. wants a verbal label for everything

4. shows no strong evidence of developmental delay, except possibly in the area of psycho-motor development; reaches most early developmental milestones on schedule

5. appears "drunk" in early attempts at walking

6. does not automatically assume a position of balance when set down after being held

7. clings to objects and other people for balance

8. constantly bumps into things (especially on the left side)

Preschool Years (3-5)

1. remarkable rote verbatim memory skills are already evident

2. is extremely verbose and may "speak like an adult" at two or three years of age

3. reading skills develop early, strong letter and number recognition, excellent spelling skills

4. makes very literal translations, sees everything as black or white

5. poor gross motor development is evident, prefers to eat and play on the floor

6. severe balance problems persist, difficulty learning to ride a tricycle

7. lack of coordination and spatial confusion leads to guarded pursuits and a fear of heights, avoids the playground jungle gym

8. simple athletic skills aren't mastered, such as throwing and catching a ball, kicking a ball, balancing on one foot, climbing monkey bars, skipping, doing jumping jacks, etc.

 The Source for Nonverbal Learning Disorder.

Preschool Years (3-5), *continued*

9.   is not drawn to building or construction toys; likes uncluttered, flat board games involving reading and/or spelling, such as Monopoly®, Scrabble®, Trivial Pursuit®, etc.

10. has poor fine-motor coordination, resists eating with silverware, has difficulty with coloring and cut-and-paste activities

11. has difficulty learning to dress; has a hard time with buttons, zippers, hooks, etc.; problems with directionality (puts clothes on backward or inside-out, shoes on the wrong feet, etc.)

12. has difficulty adjusting to transitions, responds with apprehension to new situations, prefers a set routine

13. has difficulty adjusting to a preschool setting away from the home

14. is often considered "gifted" by parents and teachers

15. avoids spontaneous social interactions, prefers playing with a single child to a group, one best friend may serve as a social guide and mentor.

16. may "overfocus" on tasks, has difficulty disengaging from any particular undertaking

Elementary Years (6-10)

1.   is frequently not yet diagnosed with NLD upon entering elementary school; often placed in gifted or accelerated programs, owing to strong verbal skills; academic achievements are seen as a strength; good reading and calculation skills

2.   works slowly; has difficulty completing tasks on time

3.   does not apply past learning to new situations; can't generalize

4.   falls out of chair when concentrating

5.   large and fine-motor problems become more pronounced, laborious handwriting, difficulty using scissors

6.   cannot tie shoelaces, difficulty using a key in a lock, talks through motor tasks

7.   talks all the time, labeled "annoying," binds through continuous dialogue

8.   has difficulty placing written responses on paper, lining up columns

9.   has weak pencil skills; all writing tasks are slow and arduous

Elementary Years (6-10), *continued*

10. has difficulty copying text from chalkboard or a book

11. makes very literal translations, often regarded as a "smart aleck"

12. makes continuous misjudgments and misinterpretations

13. has difficulty adjusting to the expectations of substitute teachers

14. is naively trusting, has no street smarts

15. may be viewed as "peculiar" or "unusual"

Middle School Years (11-14)

1. is often excluded, teased, and persecuted at school

2. is misunderstood by both teachers and peers

3. has difficulty meeting age-appropriate behavioral expectations; these difficulties may be misattributed to "emotional" issues

4. has problems with work and study habits; these problems may be misattributed to "motivational" issues

5. has visual-spatial-organizational difficulties, difficulty using a locker, can't find his way around campus, is often lost or tardy

6. as pressure to conform builds up within the child, along with normal adolescent hormonal changes, secondary emotional problems may surface; some degree of depression is not uncommon

7. makes very literal translations; has difficulty with abstract concepts; often misinterprets information, especially if relayed by means of analogies, idioms, multiple meanings, or figurative speech

8. grades go down in middle school compared to elementary school

9. in many cases, the child is first diagnosed with NLD during adolescence

24 *The Source for Nonverbal Learning Disorders*

High School Years (15-18)

1. by high school, peer tolerance usually increases; one or two close friendships may develop (or continue)

2. if an Individualized Education Program has been put into place to accommodate the student, academic achievement, which typically drops in middle school, makes an encouraging comeback; if no IEP, this student is at risk for dropping out of school

3. still thinks in concrete and literal terms

4. is slow to date and interact with the opposite sex

5. early job experience performance problems are common

6. has difficulty learning to drive, can't coordinate the use of a manual shift

7. is socially immature; may be seen as a "nerd" or "weird" by classmates

8. has low self-esteem; is prone to depression, withdrawal, anxiety, and suicide

Adulthood

1. is underemployed for level of intelligence and education

2. over-relies on rote memory; can't "wing it"

3. has problems on the job; supervisors must spell out directives

4. has problems with intimacy, inability to discern nonverbal clues, marital conflicts

5. dysfunctions associated with NLD intensify; they are not outgrown

6. serious episodes of depression often result; some cases of subsequent schizophrenia

Chapter 3
Early Adjustment Problems

The more novel the psycho-motor, visual-spatial, and/or social situation, the more evident the impairments will be . . .

Colton is a very sweet little boy I worked with more than 15 years ago, who probably meets the diagnostic criteria for NLD, but I was unfamiliar with the syndrome at that time, so I don't know if he has ever been officially diagnosed. What still stands out in my mind about Colton is his overly trusting nature. In my initial intake interview with his mother, she related the following incident to me:

> When Colton was eight, he was playing "super heroes" with some other boys around his same age. Colton wanted a turn to borrow a "Superman cape" which belonged to another boy. The boy told him: "Whoever wears this cape can really fly!"
>
> "I've never seen you fly," Colton responded reflectively, but without a trace of suspicion.
>
> "That's because you can only fly if you start from a really high place," the cunning boy replied, without missing a beat. Colton didn't notice the other youngsters around him smirking.
>
> "I'd like to fly," Colton said very sincerely.
>
> "I'll let you use my special cape," the boy agreed, "but you'll have to climb up to the top of the water tower and jump off, so you can fly down."
>
> Colton was ecstatic. He let the other boy tie the cape around his neck and he climbed to the top of the water tower. Colton never felt any sense of fear because, after all, he had been told he'd be able to fly with that special Superman cape. He spread his arms and launched himself into the air. Upon landing, Colton broke both arms, several ribs, and had to spend over a month in a full-body cast in the hospital. He was lucky to have survived.
>
> When adults questioned him afterwards, Colton kept repeating, "But they told me I'd be able to fly . . ."

Colton never questioned the motives of his "friends." You could say it was a hard way to learn a lesson, but Colton didn't learn anything from that terrible tragedy. He continued to trust everyone and to believe the things other people told him. It was as though his social radar wasn't set to pick up deception and manipulation. I hear heart-wrenching stories like Colton's over and over again from the parents of children with NLD.

Each NLD Diagnosis is Unique

The three broad aspects of development in which NLD presents deviations and abnormalities are:

1. motoric
2. visual-spatial-organizational
3. social

If a child has right hemispheric dysfunction, deficits in the three areas listed above should be quite evident to an observer during the child's early years, despite the child's valiant efforts to compensate for them. The more novel the psycho-motor, visual-spatial, and/or social situation, the more evident his impairments will be. As with any syndrome, it is important to note that not *all* of the symptoms listed here need be present in any particular child with NLD to establish that he has the disorder:

- In some children the motoric deficiencies (causing poor gross and fine motor coordination) may be more apparent.
- In some, the visual-spatial-organizational deficiencies (causing problems with aligning columns of numbers, observing directionality, and organizing work) will be the most pronounced.
- In others, the social deficiencies (causing problems with novelty and adaptive behavior) may be more noticeable.

Although a child will have particular deficits in each of the three areas, he may not show every deficit in every domain. In fact, a child will probably have developed remarkable strengths which have helped him to compensate in some realms. What is clear is that the combination of deficits found in a child with NLD will touch all aspects of day-to-day functioning, in one way or another.

Keeping this in mind, following are some of the early adjustment problems to be aware of in each category (a summary of these quandaries is included on pages 40-42 — **The Three Areas Encompassed by Nonverbal Learning Disorders**):

 The Source for Nonverbal Learning Disorders

1. Motoric

A child with NLD generally has a history of poor psycho-motor coordination. Motor clumsiness is often the first concern parents observe. Motor reaction time and speed are delayed. There may be a recognizable difference between the dominant and non-dominant sides of the body, with more noticeable problems on the left side of the body. He will avoid crossing his body midline (the imaginary line from the tip of the head to the feet, which separates the body into halves).

<table>
<tr><td>

DEFINITION

finger agnosia
  inability to interpret sensory impressions with fingers

</td></tr>
</table>

Later, in school, he may exhibit problems with dysgraphia and impaired tactile-discrimination abilities, including finger agnosia (he doesn't have the same acuity of touch in his fingers as other children do). This child's lack of motor control can manifest in social rejection, as he is constantly getting in the way, bumping into other people and objects, and is generally unaware of the position in space his body occupies. In addition to social ostracism, his motor disabilities (along with spatial misconceptions) put him at increased risk for personal injury.

As a toddler, this child will be hesitant to explore his environment motorically. Instead, he explores the world verbally by asking questions and receiving verbal answers to his questions about the environment. His motor coordination is poor, so he prefers not to move about. He doesn't explore the sensation of items on his fingers and in his mouth in the way most toddlers do. This child is missing out on a significant amount of data which is needed to form accurate impressions of the world. As a result, he won't understand the attributes and functions of the things he comes into contact with in his environment. Early sensory-motor exploration forms the basis for later learning. Because he doesn't examine and inspect objects, this child doesn't develop a visual and tactile schemata of the world.

Extreme vacillations with balance are often first evident when the child is learning to walk. He may appear "drunk" in his early attempts at walking. An unusual amount of falling will cause him to be reluctant and to cling to objects or a parent's hand to gain stabilization, long after this would normally be expected. He may also have a fear of heights and avoid climbing up on the jungle gym. It is believed that because of these deficiencies, this child receives little benefit from the sensorimotor period of development, which consequently hinders his development of higher-order concept formation, abstract reasoning, and problem-solving abilities.

Often, when the toddler with nonverbal learning disorders is set down after being held, it takes several seconds for him to

29

cognitively secure his equilibrium. As this function of the central nervous system is not integrated for him through the right hemisphere, his body will not automatically resume a position of balance. The child must literally remember a previous experience of equilibrium and then he must restructure that memory cognitively to achieve a position of bodily balance. His everyday experience is similar to the unbalanced sensation a well-integrated adult encounters when stepping off of a boat onto land after a time at sea.

> **DEFINITION**
> **sensory-motor**
>   the relationship between
>   sensation and movement

These faulty balance perceptions will make learning to ride a bike laborious beyond belief. A child with NLD takes years, not days or weeks, to conquer riding a two-wheel bicycle unaided. At the dinner table or at a desk in school, this child needs to muster an extraordinary amount of determination to remain seated in his chair. And, as soon as he diverts his attention to the task at hand (i.e., eating or school work), the cognitively maintained balance is gone, and over he topples. This child naturally prefers to eat and do school assignments on the floor, where he senses more security and support.

Simple athletic skills can't be mastered in early childhood. You may observe these difficulties:

- When this child lifts his foot to kick a soccer ball, while concentrating on the ball rather than his balance, he will subsequently lose (forget) his balance and tumble over.
- When jumping up to shoot a basket, he will not land solidly on his feet.
- When attempting to do jumping jacks, it is impossible to coordinate the two sides of his body.

The ridicule suffered by this child is catastrophic, even at the hands of possibly well-meaning coaches and P.E. teachers.

Fine motor skills are also impacted. The toddler with NLD resists eating with a spoon or fork owing to the lack of dexterity in his fingers. Learning to tie his shoelaces can take years, and he will have to talk himself through the process well into adolescence and beyond. Using scissors can be a difficult to hopeless task, as is holding a pencil correctly. This child will adapt a static tripod pencil grip and press very deeply in an attempt to control his writing, often producing dark, heavy lines. It has been said that such a child always "draws" and never actually learns to "write" (it's not too difficult to imagine the consequences this produces in school). The handwriting of the child with NLD may be quite neat, but the process remains slow and arduous for him. His daily experience with fine-motor skills has been likened to an adult who, after a stroke or being prescribed a muscle relaxant, has extreme difficulty controlling his handwriting.

The Source for Nonverbal Learning Disorders

2. Visual-Spatial-Organizational

Specific problems in this area include:

- spatial perceptions and spatial relations
- recognition, organization, and synthesis of visual-spatial information
- discrimination and recognition of visual relationships
- visual-spatial orientation (including right-left orientation problems)
- visual memories
- coordination of visual input with the motoric processes (visual-motor integration)
- visual form constancy
- gestalt processing
- concept formation

All of the above are rooted in basic deficits in visual perception and visual imagery. This child doesn't form visual images and, therefore, can't revisualize something he has seen previously. He focuses on the details of what he sees and often fails to grasp the total picture.

Visual imagery, the ability to mentally dissect what is seen and then to rearrange or reconfigure those parts in relation to the whole, like manipulating the pieces of an imaginary puzzle in your head, is paramount in our decision-making and problem-solving processes. The child with NLD wants you to always tell him what to do, tell him exactly what you expect, and tell him how to do it, because he can't figure out things for himself. He will also have difficulty following a sequence of directions or assembling a toy because he lacks the ability to create and play with visual images in his mind.

DEFINITION

gestalt perception
deriving meaning from the "whole picture," without breaking it down into parts; putting it all together; a holistic view

Visual-spatial confusion underlies many of the unusual behaviors evident in a young child with nonverbal learning disorders. This child will endeavor to "bind" to an adult, through continuous dialogue, in order to stabilize his position in a room. He needs to verbally (albeit, subconsciously) label everything that happens around him, in order to memorize and try to comprehend the everyday circumstances which others instantly and effortlessly recognize and assimilate. Experiences are stored in his memory by their verbal labels, not by visual images or by propreoceptive recall. He will have a relatively poor memory for novel or complex material or material which is not easily verbally coded.

The child with NLD must employ intense forethought to label and order everything he comes into contact with in his environment, such as counting the number of houses the bus passes on the way home from school. Owing to faulty perceptions, these labels may be incorrect, but the child perseveres because it is his only accessible means of processing the information. He doesn't form the visual images which help the rest of us to recognize and comprehend something we've seen, or a place we've been, before. This lack of ability to revisualize causes extreme difficulty for this child when trying to find his way in new places.

Spatial reference is often neglected entirely (i.e. the child may recall many distinct details of a house he has just visited, but he will not be able to describe its location in reference to other houses on the same block or to his own home; he can't conceptualize the details he has memorized in an integrated fashion to form a holistic view). He sees the veins on the leaves of the trees, but fails to see the forest. This child, naturally, is not drawn to building or construction toys.

Once in school, this student will have difficulty figuring out where and how to place written responses on a sheet of paper or how to get back to his classroom from the nurse's office. He will have problems staying with the group on a field trip or standing in his place in a line. Specific problems in arithmetic can result from deficits in visual-spatial reasoning and visual-perception. The student may have problems aligning columns of numbers, observing directionality, and organizing his work. He may be unable to visually distinguish the correct position of answers on a page or the relevant information on that page (especially if the worksheet is visually confusing). The student then becomes overloaded and overwhelmed.

The child with nonverbal learning disorders constantly talks himself through situations as a means of verbally compensating for his motoric and visual-spatial deficiencies. Although he may be unaware of the spatial position his home occupies in the neighborhood, he will find his way back from a friend's house by one or more of the following coping strategies:

- counting the homes which come in between
- labeling environmental markers
- recounting a sequence of details which he has taken pains to label and commit to verbal memory

At the mall, he may read and memorize the names of the stores he passes, but be unable to find his way out of the clothing department of a particular store.

   The Source for Nonverbal Learning Disorders

Such a child is able to achieve a limited degree of comfort in his environment through his well-developed rote memory skills. Because he can't visualize, he endeavors to remember everything and develops a remarkable memory for details. This coping technique, however, breaks down when the child encounters novel or highly complex situations. He is conditioned to prefer the security of predictable, familiar situations in which he has had some previous success. He will resist any attempts at modifying his circumstances. Tossing in a new variable to an already fairly constant situation (such as a substitute teacher taking over the control of a classroom where the child has previously gained a certain degree of stability with his regular teacher), can totally disrupt this child's coping strategies and generate an increased level of anxiety for him.

Along with graphomotor and pencil grip problems already mentioned, the child with nonverbal learning disorders may also have difficulty remembering the shapes of letters (visual memory) and using the correct sequence of strokes to form letters (visual-sequential memory). He will have difficulty with the concept of visual form constancy; the ability to perceive that an object possesses unchanging properties, such as specific shape, position and size, in various representations of its image. All writing tasks will be slow and arduous. Copying accurately from the board or a book are impractical and agonizing for this child.

3. Social

Deficits in social awareness and social judgment, though the child is struggling to fit in and his actions are certainly not deliberate, will often be misinterpreted as "annoying" or "attention-getting" by adults and peers alike. It is clear that these students are motivated to conform and adapt socially, but sadly, they *perceive* and *interpret* social situations inaccurately. The blunders committed are usually not flagrant in nature, but rather incessant and tenacious; hence the label "annoying." Social competence disabilities are an integral component of the NLD syndrome and this aspect of the impairment may lead to an overdependence upon adults (especially parents).

The social indiscretions frequently committed by the child with NLD represent his inability to discern or process perceptual cues in communication. He will not pick up information from his surroundings the way other children do. The aforementioned visual-spatial-organizational deficits cause him to be ineffective at recognizing faces, interpreting gestures, deciphering postural clues, and reading facial expressions. Conventions governing physical proximity and distance are also not perceived. Changes in tone or pitch of voice or emphasis of delivery aren't noticed or distinguished. Likewise, this child won't appropriately alter his expression and elocution in speech. This can be evidenced in what may appear to be terse or curt response styles.

DENNIS THE MENACE

"BOY, IF YOU DON'T KNOW WHAT MARGARET'S THINKING ABOUT, YOU'RE NOT LISTENING."

"Dennis the Menace" used by permission of Hank Ketchum and © by North America Syndicate.

The importance of nonverbal signals and cues was noted previously, and it has been shown that more than 65% of the intent of an average conversation is conveyed nonverbally. However, the child with nonverbal learning disorders will try to resolve all quandaries by employing his strong verbal skills and using his strong memory. He has to piece together the meaning of a conversation or directive from the approximately 35% (verbal) that he actually receives and processes. A lot of the behavioral incompetencies observed in a child with NLD result from the fact that he truly does not understand what is happening or what is expected of him. He totally misses the majority of relevant content which is being conveyed nonverbally and, as a result, much of his conversational responses don't fit with the tone and mood of the occasion. This child is likely to become withdrawn in novel social situations or to appear out of place.

The impairments of NLD also lead to a preponderance of very literal translations, which, in turn, precede continuous misjudgments and misinterpretations. Some poignant examples of literal translations follow:

Damon

Remember Damon from Chapter 1? His mother recalls a time when he was five years old and she dropped him off to play at his cousin Michael's house. Michael was the same age as Damon and they often played together. While they played, it became very windy outside, so Damon's aunt helped him put on one of his cousin's sweatshirts. When Damon's mother returned to pick him up, he was glad to see her and rushed into her arms.

"You'll have to take Michael's sweatshirt off before we go," his mother told Damon. And then, before she could say anything further, Damon ran up to Michael and began pulling on the sweatshirt that Michael was wearing.

"He's doing exactly what you asked him to," Damon's aunt laughed.

Damon's mother then tried to explain to him that she meant he needed to take off the sweatshirt belonging to

Michael that he had borrowed and was currently wearing. Such a detailed explanation would not have been necessary for another five-year-old, but for Damon, who always took the most literal translation of anything said, his mother was accustomed to rephrasing her instructions. And, it was just this sort of very literal translation that was already starting to cause problems in school for Damon.

Kirsten

Six-year-old Kirsten's grandparents were baby-sitting her while she was home from school with the flu. She was a precocious child whose NLD was not diagnosed until a number of years later. Her grandmother went to check on Kirsten in her bedroom and said, "Grandpa is in the den if you need anything. I'm going to run down to the grocery store to buy some eggs. I should be back in 10 or 15 minutes."

"But, Grandma," Kirsten sounded perplexed, "why don't you take the car, instead of running all the way there?"

Her grandmother thought the remark was cute, but took the time to explain to Kirsten that she wasn't really going to "run," that it was just an expression she used sometimes. Kirsten's literal assumptions about expressions were earning her a reputation as a smart aleck in her first grade classroom, where her teacher had a low tolerance level for that type of "silliness."

Cody

In another instance, four-year-old Cody was playing in his daycare sandbox when a group of children started putting sand in each other's hair. The childcare worker spotted Cody dumping a handful of sand in Jennifer's hair.

"Cody! Don't put sand in Jennifer's hair!" she screeched.

"Okay," Cody promised, as he proceeded to drop a handful of sand in Joshua's hair.

The childcare worker grabbed Cody by the arm, shouting, "I just finished telling you not to do that!"

"No, you didn't," Cody protested matter-of-factly. "You told me not to put sand in Jennifer's hair."

"You knew what I meant!" the childcare worker persisted indignantly.

"How could I know what you meant?" Cody looked bewildered.

His last question was ignored and he was sent inside to time out for the rest of the afternoon. Cody's face was bathed in tears when his mother arrived for him a couple of hours later. Cody's mother tried to explain to the childcare worker that Cody always took things literally and that he didn't mean to be defiant.

However, the childcare worker responded by stating that Cody would have to "stop taking things literally" around her (in other words, she insisted that he "read her mind"). Although Cody was receiving occupational therapy for his coordination problems, his NLD would not be correctly diagnosed for years to come.

Lindsay

Five-year-old Lindsay always seemed to be confused by rhetorical questions

When her mother would say, "Would you like to pick up your toys now?" Lindsay would say "No!"

Then Lindsay's mother would caution her, "Don't talk to me like that!" To which Lindsay would reply, "I was just answering your question."

After several such confrontations, her mother explained to Lindsay, "Sometimes I ask a question, as a polite way of making a request." Lindsay responded to this disclosure by beseeching her mother, "Will you please tell me first when you are going to do that?"

If Lindsay hadn't sounded so sincere, her mother probably would have thought she was being flippant. Instead, Lindsay's candor prompted her mother's long search to find out why her daughter needed so many things explained to her that all the other children seemed to grasp intuitively. Lindsay was diagnosed with NLD four years later.

Bradley

In school, Bradley was known as the clown of his second grade class. One day, at the conclusion of a sustained silent reading period, the teacher flipped the lights off and on again quickly. This nonverbal action was her signal to the class that it was time for the students to put their books away. Despite the lights blinking on and off,

Bradley continued reading. His teacher, weary of the long arguments she often had to engage in with Bradley, stood quietly behind him and cleared her throat a few times. The other students giggled nervously, but Bradley continued reading.

Finally, the teacher exclaimed in a very authoritative tone, "If I were you, I'd put that book away right NOW!"

But Bradley continued to read. Before he knew what hit him, he was dragged out of the room and sent to the office with a referral to the principal for "defiant" behavior. The teacher wrote on the form that "after several warnings, Bradley defiantly refused to put his book away." Bradley insisted to the principal that he had not been defiant, that his teacher had never asked him to put his book away, she had merely stated what she would do, if she were him. Bradley received a detention, because no one at the school understood that he was unable to pick up the teacher's nonverbal cues (flipping the lights off and on, clearing her throat, elevating the tone of her voice), and that he had translated her statement of what she would do as a literal statement, not a request. He also failed to notice that all of the other students had already put their books away.

Bradley was, of course, correct when he stated that his teacher never asked him to put his book away. Given his mode of very literal interpretation, she hadn't. According to her, she most emphatically had. Bradley was labeled "passive-resistive" by the school staff and often disciplined. Each time he was scolded, Bradley insisted that he had done nothing wrong. Bradley complained to his parents that the adults at his school treated him very unfairly. Finally, in the third grade, Bradley was referred for assessment and diagnosed as meeting the criteria of a nonverbal learning disorder. An incredible amount of psychological damage had been inflicted on him by that time by those who should have been more aware.

Melanie

Six-year-old Melanie is another child with NLD who tends to take everything said in its most literal context. When her mother asked Melanie if she could "keep an eye on our food" at a family picnic, Melanie went screaming off to her father.

"I don't want to put my eye on our food," Melanie protested, when her mother tried to figure out what had set her off this time. Taking the time to decipher the child's interpretation can aid you in helping her to adjust.

If you find yourself saying, "That's just an expression, what I really meant was . . ." constantly throughout the day, you are dealing with a child who makes very literal interpretations of everything she hears and is unable to decipher other meanings. Rather than avoid idiomatic expressions, point them out when you use them, explain them, and build up the child's competence.

Other Social Traits to Look For

The child with NLD is naively trusting of others (to a fault) and doesn't embrace the concept of dishonesty (even in terms of small lies) or of withholding (even inflammatory) information. He won't recognize when he is being lied to or deceived by others. Deceit, cunning, and manipulation are beyond this child's scope of interpretation. He assumes that everyone is friendly who displays that front verbally and that the intentions of others are only that which they expose verbally. As was illustrated in Colton's catastrophe, an inability to read the intentions of others often results in a lot of unfortunate scapegoating of the child. He needs to be *taught* to question the motives of others; he won't learn from experience.

A child with nonverbal learning disorders is very concrete in his translations, expression, and outlook of the world. His social relationships tend to be routinized and stereotypical. Because he doesn't automatically adjust to changes in his environment, he finds comfort in ritualization. He likes things to stay the same and to be done in the same order every time. After his first swimming lesson at age six, Colton's mother stopped to get him an ice cream cone on the way home. From then on, stopping for an ice cream cone became part of the ritual. Colton expected that every day after swimming, he would get his ice cream. His mother learned to be careful of spur-of-the-moment decisions, because they often became rituals that Colton was reluctant to relinquish.

And this child sees everything in terms of black or white — true or false. Hidden meanings have to be pointed out because they won't be intuitively detected or conceived. A child with NLD might be regarded as a smart aleck (as with Cody, Lindsay, Bradley, and most of the others) because of constant misinterpretations of the language he hears. He is frequently reprimanded with the words, "You knew what I meant!" The child, of course, didn't have a clue about what was meant and has no way to access what is meant, but not actually said.

Perceptual cues serve in the same capacity as traffic signals — they govern the flow, give-and-take, and fluctuations in our conversations. The child who can't read these nonverbal cues is frequently determined to be ill-mannered, discourteous, curt, immature, lacking in respect for others, self-centered, or even defiant. The child with NLD is none of the above. Like the color-blind driver who can't respond appropriately to traffic lights, this is a child who is utilizing all of the resources available to him in order to try to make sense of a world which is providing him with faulty cues and unreliable information.

It is currently difficult to locate a professional who understands non-verbal learning disorders, but such professionals do exist. If a child exhibits the developmental deficiencies described above, he can be helped to lead an easier, less troublesome life. An effective intervention approach incorporates constantly and explicitly spelling out to this child what other children would be able to pick up or infer intuitively. Any intervention strategies should include a strong verbal component because that is the only way the child will process and assimilate accurate observations of his environment.

The Three Areas Encompassed by Nonverbal Learning Disorders

1. Motoric

- ❑ poor psycho-motor coordination
- ❑ difference between dominant and non-dominant sides of body
- ❑ problems on left side of body
- ❑ avoids crossing midline
- ❑ hesitant to explore motorically
- ❑ extreme vascillations with balance
- ❑ cognitively secures equilibrium
- ❑ doesn't automatically resume balance
- ❑ learning to ride a bike takes *years*
- ❑ difficult to remain seated in chair
- ❑ prefers to eat and work on the floor
- ❑ simple athletic skills aren't mastered
- ❑ difficulty with fine motor skills
- ❑ resists eating with a spoon or fork
- ❑ difficulty learning to tie shoes
- ❑ talks himself through motor tasks
- ❑ difficulty using scissors
- ❑ difficulty holding a pencil correctly
- ❑ presses very deeply to control writing

     The Source for Nonverbal Learning Disorders

2. Visual-Spatial-Organizational

- ❑ difficulty with spatial perceptions and spatial relations

- ❑ difficulty with recognition and organization of visual-spatial information

- ❑ difficulty with visual memory and visualization

- ❑ difficulty with coordination of visual input with motoric processes

- ❑ difficulty with visual form constancy

- ❑ difficulty with gestalt impressions

- ❑ difficulty with concept formation

- ❑ problems with visual-spatial confusion

- ❑ "binds" through continuous dialogue

- ❑ verbally labels everything

- ❑ doesn't form visual images or revisualize

- ❑ spatial reference is neglected

- ❑ not drawn to building or construction toys

- ❑ difficulty placing written responses

- ❑ difficulty maneuvering through space

- ❑ talks himself/herself through space

- ❑ uses counting, labeling, recounting

- ❑ prefers predictable situations

- ❑ difficulty remembering shapes

- ❑ difficulty remembering sequence

- ❑ all writing tasks are slow and arduous

- ❑ difficulty copying from chalkboard

3. Social

❑   labeled "annoying" or "attention-getting"

❑   social blunders are incessant and tenacious

❑   inability to discern nonverbal cues

❑   ineffective at recognizing faces

❑   ineffective at interpreting gestures

❑   ineffective at deciphering postural clues

❑   ineffective at reading facial expressions

❑   does not notice changes in tone of voice

❑   does not alter expression in speech

❑   terse or curt responses

❑   very literal translations

❑   continuous social misjudgments and misinterpretations

❑   naively trusting

❑   does not understand deceit, cunning, or manipulation

❑   takes everyone at face value

❑   concrete outlook of the world

❑   hidden meanings in language and social interactions aren't detected

❑   often regarded as a "smart aleck"

❑   seen as ill-mannered, discourteous, rude

                                    The Source for Nonverbal Learning Disorders

Chapter 4
Diagnosing and Servicing Nonverbal Learning Disorders

The incredible rote memory which served this child very well in the lower grades, fails him when academic demands shift to more complex applications . . .

Joseph can talk your ear off. Not only does he have something to say about everything, but he actually seems to know something about everything! His varied interests include music, computers, space travel, and ice hockey. Joseph is also a trivia buff, memorizing obscure details that amaze and daunt his acquaintances. He has a strong memory for everything he has ever heard. The way Joseph stores and retrieves information calls to mind the capacities of a super computer.

A slender boy with silky black hair, whose body language is shy and withdrawn, his marked verbosity tends to surprise the casual observer. Despite his talkative nature, Joseph is a sensitive child who resists change and has difficulty making friends. Joseph's mother is a Russian immigrant and his father, a third-generation Chinese American. Both parents hail from cultures which place a marked emphasis on formal education. Good grades and scholastic achievement have always been highly regarded in Joseph's home.

Early on, Joseph didn't disappoint his parents. He earned several academic awards, including the county spelling bee champ, by the time he reached the third grade. That same year, the lead role of the school play was given to Joseph, because his teacher knew he would have no difficulty memorizing every line. Although his delivery was somewhat flat, adults were impressed that he could recite such a difficult script, seemingly without effort. But Joseph seemed to have a gift for repeating back lengthy conversations verbatim. Joseph's parents were always enthralled by his ability to mimic discussions, word-for-word, exactly as they were spoken. His early grades were excellent, until third grade, when Joseph began having difficulty completing his written assignments and projects.

"It's not fair," Joseph would often protest. "It takes me four times as long as anyone else to finish my work."

"Don't complain," his parents would say. "You are one of the top students in your class!"

Nonverbal learning disorders are often overlooked educationally, because the student is, as a means of compensating, very verbal. He has a highly developed memory for rote verbal information, so early reading and spelling skills constitute a strong domain. This child will remember every word he hears and develop a spectacular vocabulary. At times, he may appear not to be listening, but he will still be able to repeat back, verbatim, everything that has been said. However, if this child doesn't hear the whole message (i.e., the teacher turns her back momentarily), he won't infer the information that is missing, even if he has heard the major essence of the words. He can't fill in the blanks.

Tools and Measures for a Diagnosis

NLD doesn't consist of a precise mold that a child either fits perfectly into or he doesn't. There is a wide range of behaviors and abilities which present themselves in a child with white matter dysfunction. It is important to look back and determine if these behaviors are chronic. If you observe a significant number of the early adjustment problems detailed in Chapter 3 (and on the checklists on pages 40-42) in a child, an intelligence screening may support your suspicions that this child is overly dependent upon his verbal skills and has limited access to his nonverbal skills.

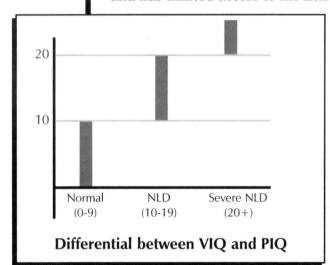

Differential between VIQ and PIQ

Normal	NLD	Severe NLD
(0-9)	(10-19)	(20+)

An IQ measure, such as the WISC-III, which reveals a performance IQ (PIQ) scale score depressed (by 10 points or more) relative to the student's verbal IQ (VIQ) score, may denote a deficient right-hemisphere system. It is not relevant to the diagnostic process whether one or both of these scores is above or below the norm; the crucial determinant is the relative discrepancy between the VIQ and PIQ. It is not unusual for a child with nonverbal learning disabilities to have a VIQ in the very superior range. When subtest scores are grouped, the verbal conceptualization cluster will generally be the strongest for the child with NLD, while the spatial cluster will be the weakest.

Depending upon the severity of the disorder, and also upon the child's intelligence and the coping techniques which he has already put into place, the discrepancy can be 20 points or more. Such a discrepancy is severe and warrants immediate attention, no matter what the child's full-scale IQ (FSIQ). You aren't merely discovering that the child has a dominance of the left cerebral hemisphere, but rather that he is having

44   *The Source for Nonverbal Learning Disorders*

difficulty accessing the processes specialized in the right cerebral hemisphere. A 10-15 point discrepancy is considered significant on most measures.

Proper diagnosis is important because only then can parents, educators and therapists develop a specific intervention plan to service the child with NLD. But the correct diagnosis may be a long time in coming. NLD is totally invisible to the casual observer:

- There is no immediate impression of a disability.
- The child is probably comely, bright, and extremely articulate.
- His outward appearance is no different from that of his classmates.
- He may seem precocious among his peers.
- His skills may look to be right on target, until a deeper look reveals that he is putting in a tremendous effort to front this appearance of "normality."

It takes an experienced professional to pick the child with NLD out of the line-up!

DEFINITION

Intervention Based Multifactored Evaluation
a collaborative, problem-solving process which focuses on concerns which affect the learner's educational progress within a learning environment

The assessment of individuals suspected to have NLD should be conducted by an interdisciplinary team and focused toward developing an appropriate intervention plan. There is no single test, there are no clusters of tests, there is no cut-off score on an individual test that, in and of itself, will signal the presence of NLD. It is important for the child's parents to be involved at all levels of an Intervention Based Multifactored Evaluation process. The most crucial consideration when retaining professionals for an evaluation of your child is that they be knowledgeable of NLD and that they know how to distinguish it from other disorders with the same or similar symptoms. (A discussion of NLD and related disorders makes up Chapter 12.)

It is imperative to understand the meaning of a child's assessment through a profile of all the test scores, a profile of specific strengths and weaknesses as they relate to the child's current difficulties, and a developmental profile of functional abilities. A comprehensive assessment battery would include the following components:

- a thorough developmental history
- neuropsychological testing
- a speech and language evaluation
- educational assessments
- occupational therapy evaluation

Parents may want to go over all of these findings with an educational consultant at the conclusion of the assessment process.

Some of the professionals who might be involved in the diagnostic process include the following:

- a developmental pediatrician
- a pediatric neurologist
- a neuropsychologist
- a speech and language pathologist
- an educational therapist

In addition, these professionals might also play a role in diagnosing NLD:

- A pediatric audiologist may uncover some right-hemisphere deficiencies while evaluating the child's auditory processing.
- A developmental optometrist is trained to spot some of the visual-spatial disturbances which accompany NLD.
- An occupational therapist can assesses the developmental coordination and fine-motor problems which occur.

The child's overall ability to function in life should be considered over any individual test scores. The interrelationship between data and the patterns which elucidate how the child arrived at his responses are more important than the individual data itself in helping to fully understand this child. An educational therapist can synthesize all evaluation findings into a single, coherent profile of the child and consult with parents about what steps to take next. In this way, succinct and realistic intervention recommendations can be provided.

Be careful that the final report is not merely a description of the child's scores on various tests, which will not necessarily tell you anything about that particular child. Test scores won't and can't reveal everything that is going on with a child with NLD. Teachers and parents can't possibly receive an adequate understanding of the severity of NLD or develop an appropriate approach to intervention from a handful of test scores. Evaluators *must compile critical observations* of how the child works through a problem, not simply data that shows if he got the answer right or wrong. A child can use a small area of strength (such as item by item analysis) to surmount an enormous area of deficiency (such as visual-motor integration). On the other hand, this same child can be working in his absolute area of strength and one marginal deficit will throw him totally off track. Unless the examiner observes the child's process, all he or she will end up with is a meaningless score. Interpretation of all scores is relational.

If the evaluators don't watch and take note of the child's problem-solving abilities, they can't possibly develop an appropriate plan for intervention. An Intervention-Based Multifactored Evaluation yields the kind of information that therapists, teachers, and parents need in order to plan and implement effective interventions. It "is an approach which places primary emphasis on identifying and solving a student's educational and adjustment difficulties." The Intervention-Based Multifactored Evaluation process is geared toward understanding pragmatic difficulties, primarily identified by parents and teachers, which affect the child's learning and adjustment. This allows intervention plans to be developed which will match this individual's needs.

What Happens After NLD is Diagnosed?

Once a child has been properly diagnosed, parents should not accept the rationale of some well-meaning professionals who may tell them that NLD will play a minor role in their child's ability to perform well in school. Physicians and psychologists may assume that a child with superior expressive language skills can easily compensate for a deficit in nonverbal skills. This assumption is true only in relation to the child's capacity to "parrot" back school work in the early grades and doesn't address the child's inability to flow through life. NLD is a serious and debilitating syndrome which significantly impairs an individual's adaptive functioning.

C ompensations

A ccommodations

M odifications

S trategies

As the child moves into the higher grades, where less and less will be spelled out for him, he will reach a point where functioning in school is impossible without specific compensations, accommodations, modifications and strategies (CAMS). The incredible rote memory which served this child very well in the lower grades, before he was being asked to interpret and assess information, fails him when academic demands shift to more complex applications. His system begins to break down when he is asked to evaluate or reorder the information he has memorized, and to form his own original thoughts.

At this point, he may cease to try or "burn out" attempting to succeed under the impossible demands now being placed upon him. Recognizing this eventuality and employing interventions early in the child's schooling is certainly preferable to waiting until junior or senior high to accommodate this syndrome, when he finally bottoms out. Early implementation of CAMS will maximize his success in school. Unless appropriate CAMS are initiated during the elementary years, long-term prognosis for success in school is poor for this child. (Chapter 8 contains CAMS specific to the child with NLD.)

The transition from elementary school to junior high was a traumatic one for Joseph. When he turned 12, Joseph began refusing to go to school. He told his parents he was being bullied by some eighth grade boys because of his Chinese ancestry (his interpretation of the situation). Joseph was constantly teased by his classmates and called a "nerd." Gang members beat him up for wearing the wrong colors to school. He couldn't figure out why he was always the victim of everyone's pranks. Even his teachers seemed to pick on him.

Eventually, going to school became a waking nightmare that Joseph could no longer endure. With trepidation, his parents allowed him to stay home for a few days while they attempted to work things out with the school staff. His father immediately met with school officials. They assured him that the staff would remain alert for racially-motivated incidents. Then they shocked Joseph's father by telling him that Joseph was currently failing in most of his classes, due to what they labeled "laziness." But Joseph's father knew that Joseph had been staying up half the night working on his homework; he couldn't figure out how such an obviously bright student as Joseph could possibly be so far behind.

Meanwhile, Joseph stayed home from school, working on his computer and watching TV. He barricaded himself in his bedroom and refused to see his friends. Joseph wanted to return to school, but he was afraid — afraid of his teachers, afraid of the other students, and afraid of the immense amount of written work. He knew he couldn't meet the demands being placed upon him, but felt he should be able to complete the same amount of school work as his peers. For Joseph, there simply weren't enough hours in the day for him to finish all of the written assignments required, even if he worked all day and all night. And yet, his peers, many of whom he knew to be less intelligent than him, seemed to breeze right through these same written assignments.

Special education services were not considered for Joseph at that time because of his strong verbal skills and early academic successes. Many of the parents of children with NLD that I have spoken with report having taken their children out of public school for varying lengths of time in order to shelter them from the emotional abuse they suffer at school as the consequences of this syndrome catch up with them. This time away from school currently seems to be a necessary step for the child's emotional survival in a number of cases where the school officials are unwilling or unable to recognize and accommodate the child's nonverbal learning disorders. The inconsistencies in the child's academic and social performance reflect real learning difficulties, not laziness!

Secondary Complications of NLD

A child with NLD is especially inclined toward developing depression and/or anxiety disorders if his nonverbal learning disorders are not recognized early and accommodated in a compassionate, responsible, and supportive fashion by everyone involved in his life. If the child is continually being told by the adults around him, "You could do better, if you really tried," or "You're just not applying yourself" (both false observations in this case), his level of frustration will naturally intensify and his self-image will plummet. He then develops a negative view of himself, the world, and his future.

It isn't unusual for a child with nonverbal learning disorders to become increasingly isolated and withdrawn, as failures in school multiply and intensify. Like Joseph, this child may become a loner and withdraw from contacts with his friends and the outside world. Or, like Keisha from Chapter 2, she may become passive, shut down, and refuse to put any effort into anything. These are a couple of the prevalent coping strategies these children employ as they turn inward, when the adults around them fail to recognize and accommodate their nonverbal learning disorders.

As the child becomes more and more frustrated, he may be treated for the secondary emotional issues which have developed, and which now overshadow the underlying cause (which is, of course, his nonverbal learning disorders). In almost all of the NLD cases I have encountered until recently, emotional issues have had to be addressed at some point. Under-recognition of NLD in schools appears to be a rampant problem. Misdiagnosis, or an incomplete diagnosis (many learning disorders have a co-morbid relation), will only serve to compound the problems a child is experiencing. It isn't uncommon for a child with nonverbal learning disorders to be misdiagnosed with conditions such as attention deficit disorder or emotional disturbance. In many aspects, the NLD syndrome resembles AD/HD (see the chart on page 54), but the attention deficit is specific to the visual and tactile modalities. The child with NLD doesn't have primary attention deficits or emotional issues.

NLD Interventions in the School Setting

Even when a child has been correctly diagnosed with NLD, as Joseph eventually was, it may still be difficult for him to receive the program modifications and accommodations he needs in school. After all, he is probably performing at or above grade level on most academic achievement tasks which are routinely measured at school, especially during the early elementary years. Although the deficits in motor, visual-spatial-organizational and social skills may be obvious to any interested and observant person, these impairments will not necessarily evoke the concern or compassion of any but the most caring of teachers.

If the formula for language-based (specific) learning disabilities is called upon, parents may be told that their child doesn't qualify for special

crystallized intelligence
storehouse of general information/knowledge; overlearned skills; rote, "old" learning; information based on past learning

education services because there isn't a severe discrepancy between the child's potential and his achievement in academic areas. In fact, the child's level of accomplishment in academics may even appear to go *beyond* his potential, if the measurement techniques are largely verbal (oral/written), relying upon crystallized intelligence. "Overlearning" is common among individuals with the NLD syndrome. They have strong crystallized intelligence and weak fluid intelligence.

Nonverbal learning disorders constitute a dysfunction in the basic cerebral processes and, as such, denote a disability which warrants specialized support and program modifications for the student Since this child's condition seriously interferes with his ability to perform in school, an Individualized Education Program (IEP) can, and should be, developed for him and implemented throughout the school day. Or, since this child's NLD impairments "substantially limit one or more major life activities," a 504 Plan can be drawn up to help define appropriate accommodations for him.

504 Plan
Section 504 of PL 93-112 (The Rehabilitation Act of 1973) defines a disabled individual as anyone who experiences a "mental, psychological, or physiologic disorder which interferes with [that] individual's civil right to do one or more major life activities." If a student has a disabling condition which interferes with his ability to learn or perform up to his ability in school, the school district must draw up a plan of appropriate CAMS to be implemented for this student. All special education students covered under PL 92-142 (IDEA) are automatically covered under Section 504 of PL 93-112. An IEP can serve in place of a 504 plan.

Often, the child with NLD will have already been mislabeled by unenlightened adults at his school. Today, thankfully, intelligent parents are not so quick to accept some educators' misguided declarations that their child is "lazy," "purposefully disruptive," "a troublemaker," "disturbed," "defiant," or merely "being annoying," as if these presentations were a diagnosis rather than an indicator of symptoms to be considered within the context of a syndrome. It is always wise to locate the underlying cause of behavioral observations (i.e., a disorder of the central nervous system), so that appropriate, helpful, and non-punitive measures can be implemented, knowing that the child's behavior isn't deliberate and that his mistakes and misdeeds are the result of this syndrome and are unintentional on his part. Noncompetence should never be treated as though it were noncompliance.

Joseph's parents met a lot of resistance from the staff at his school, even after Joseph had been correctly diagnosed as meeting the criteria for NLD. Their district special education staff didn't want to provide special education services for a child they felt was capable of succeeding on his own. The special education department felt Joseph would be fine if he would just "pull himself together." His teachers concluded that Joseph couldn't possibly have a serious learning disability, because the work he did complete was outstanding. They wanted to push him to do more and force him to take responsibility for his failures. It sounded reasonable enough, but was, in fact, the most destructive approach imaginable for Joseph.

To many observers, it seems incongruent that a child who speaks like an adult, reads far beyond his grade level, and wins spelling bee championships can't finish a simple written paragraph, do a jumping jack, or comprehend the meaning of nonverbal cues (as was the case with Joseph). But, when the other children his age were exploring their world motorically and observing the intricacies of social interaction, the child with NLD was relying upon the part of his brain available to him to overdevelop his vocabulary and symbolic language skills. These highly evolved language skills create an *illusion of competency* in a child who lags far behind his peers in many respects.

Parents should be especially leery of self-righteous educators who use the superficial psycho-babble "he chose," implying that this child has made a conscious choice to put himself in a position of disadvantage. No child *chooses* to fail. If a child exhibits the features of the NLD syndrome, it is important for everyone to understand that his impairments are neurologically-based in nature and there is no choice involved for that child. It is human nature to seek out the acceptance, approval, and recognition of others. To dismiss or label the adjustment problems of NLD (which are symptoms) as willful attention-getting behavior, is as harmful as it is unprofessional.

Renowned pediatrician Mel Levine states:

> "From the moment school-age children emerge from the bed covers each day until their safe return to that security, they are preoccupied with the avoidance of humiliation at all cost. They have the constant need to look good, to sidestep embarrassment, and to gain respect, especially from their peers."

Classroom Intervention

The child with NLD can usually be accommodated in an inclusive educational setting, if his unique academic and social needs are understood by his parents and his school staff. A comprehensive and detailed Individualized Education Program (IEP), put together by a team of informed experts, will aid in a successful outcome. The more extensive the IEP, the less likely it is that the child will encounter unforeseen roadblocks or fall through the cracks. He may also benefit from some special education support services, such as speech and language therapy for deficiencies in linguistic pragmatics and occupational therapy for gross and fine-motor skill concerns.

All too often though, the coping behaviors of the child with NLD are misinterpreted by uninformed adults as emotional or motivational problems. However, when this child's verbal strengths are capitalized upon, and his teachers are flexible and receptive to his needs, he can be quite successful in a regular school setting. It is so easy for adults to punish and to try to put the responsibility back on the child, but a true professional will recognize that if a child is not fulfilling their expectations, it is due to faulty planning on the part of the educational team, and is in no way a reflection on the child.

Psychotherapy

Although often suggested, "insight-oriented" dynamic psychotherapy has proven to be counterproductive as a model of intervention for an individual with NLD and is not advised. Individuals with NLD are often assumed to be very perceptive because they display well-developed verbal skills. Since their symptomology can appear to be emotionally-based, insight-oriented psychotherapy is frequently attempted. Dr. Byron P. Rourke has found that formal educational intervention is the treatment modality most likely to "increase the NLD youngster's probability of success." Treatment within a class or center for the emotionally disturbed (as was suggested for Keisha) also isn't recommended, as therapeutic approaches to emotional problems are quite different from those which have proven effective for the NLD syndrome.

The Important Role Parents Play

The parents of a child with NLD have probably already gained an intuitive or learned appreciation of what works best for their particular child. Often this child prospers at home, because of his parents' insightful adaptive strategies, while continuing to struggle at school. Parents that follow their instincts, letting the responses of their child be their guide, often develop effective strategies that will work at home, at school, and in the community. It is wise for educators to benefit from the knowledge that these parents can offer regarding their child. They can usually adapt the same strategies that have worked at home for more success in the classroom setting. School staff and parents should work closely together in planning to accommodate the child's unique needs.

52 *The Source for Nonverbal Learning Disorders*

Integrating an Intervention Approach

The child with NLD requires individualized approaches to educational intervention in order to succeed in school because his right hemisphere functions are inaccessible to him. The left cerebral hemisphere processes information based upon fixed systems of rules and isn't equipped to deal flexibly with decision-making and problem-solving strategies. The set of deficits underlying the disorder will present differently for each child with nonverbal learning disabilities. Effective intervention methods include *direct verbal training* in the following areas:

- planning
- discriminating
- temporal concepts
- organizational skills
- study skills
- written expression
- body image
- social cognition
- interpersonal communication

Encourage compensations that rely upon the child's strong rote memory and eliminate stressful situations (frequent changes, timed-tests, long written assignments, visual-spatial projects, and activities requiring intact fine and gross motor skills) at school.

Unlike an Individualized Education Program, in which the primary goal is to master a continuum of curricular skills, the educational plan for the child with NLD should consist of providing additional coping skills, practical support and CAMS. Since the means by which learning becomes impeded for this child is very different from a child with a language-based learning disability, the approach toward intervention differs also. Remember, the IEP is supposed to be focused on the needs of the child. Interventions for this child are not curative in nature, but rather designed to offer compensatory techniques, and to lessen the daily stress he encounters. Some of the specific compensations, accommodations, modifications, and strategies which should be employed to help this child can be found in Chapter 7.

Comparison of AD/HD and NLD

AD/HD	NLD
often fidgets or squirms	constantly bumping into objects
difficulty remaining still/seated	difficulty maintaining balance in seat
easily distracted	faulty spatial perceptions
difficulty waiting turns/pushes	difficulty with spatial relations/bumps
often blurts out answers	does not censor speech
difficulty following through	slow/arduous performance of tasks
does not consider consequences	does not anticipate consequences
difficulty sustaining attention	attention deficits to visual/tactile
difficulty playing quietly	talks through all activities
often talks excessively	very verbal (unless withdrawn)
often interrupts or intrudes	deficits in social judgment
does not seem to listen	misreads nonverbal communication
loses things necessary for tasks	visual-spatial-organizational deficits
engages in dangerous activities	at increased risk for personal injury
shifts from one activity to another	extraordinary attention to detail (hyper-focused)
manipulates situations	cannot comprehend personal manipulation or deception
oppositional/defiant behavior	inclined towards depression/anxiety
seeks out novelty/surprise/newness	avoids any kind of novelty

   The Source for Nonverbal Learning Disorders

Chapter 5

Helping the Child with
Nonverbal Learning Disorders at Home

> *It is advantageous to attempt to create a caring, protective*
> *environment at home for the child with NLD . . .*

Eleven-year-old Katie's mother describes her as overly anxious, a "born worrier." A talkative little redhead with a permanent pout, she is extremely self-critical and perfectionistic. From early on, nothing she did ever seemed to live up to her self-imposed high standards of exactitude. By fifth grade, Katie became so anxious about her school work, she would stay up all night. She spent hours going over every detail of her assignments, never quite finishing what she set out to accomplish in the first place. Katie would crumple up numerous papers and, in the end, have little or nothing to show for her hours of work.

Katie's mother took to calling her a worrywart. This incensed Katie, who didn't take well to familial teasing. In fact, Katie always became extremely distressed by any kind of ribbing or sarcasm. She exhibited a low level of tolerance for frustration and she tended to overreact to the comments of others. It seemed impossible for her to take part in light-hearted social chit-chat or back-and-forth bantering. Everything was serious business with Katie. And, she always took everything anyone said in its most literal context.

"Why am I so stupid?" Katie would scream at her mother, constantly chastising her own insignificant mistakes.

Her mother knew that Katie wasn't stupid. The school work she did complete usually earned top grades. It was just that Katie rarely completed an assignment. By the time any particular task met Katie's self-approval, it was frequently long past the due date. Katie's mother watched her strange pencil grip and the way she pressed through several sheets of paper and wondered why she didn't just "lighten up." Katie's whole approach to life was so tense and so intense. Her mediocre grades didn't reflect the preposterous amount of time she spent mulling over her school assignments.

The extreme attention to detail exhibited by a child with NLD can lead to a high level of accuracy and neatness, which often masks the amount of difficulty she actually had producing the work. The problem seen in a child with NLD, like Katie, is not obsessive-compulsiveness or perseverance, but rather it is brought about by too much attention to detail and an inability to see the whole picture. She never does things just to get them done. This is not the child you want to tell to "always do your best." She will, quite literally, attempt to always do her best . . . and never finish anything.

As you can see in all of the children with NLD profiled in this book, each one is unique and displays a slightly different combination of adjustment problems. Despite their differences, three major areas of developmental deviations and abnormalities are consistently present:

- motoric
- visual-spatial-organizational
- social

As a parent, you will observe a large variety of day-to-day manifestations which denote your child's lack of competence in the areas above. No matter how your child's NLD presents itself, it will probably become obvious to you early on that unique parenting styles and methods are essential to parent this child. Expect to spend a tremendous amount of time verbalizing to your child the things that other children intuit. And, remember to use your child's verbal strengths to support her weaker areas.

A Parent's Acceptance

Regardless of how or when your child is first diagnosed with NLD, the revelation usually generates a lot of mixed emotions. Initially, you will probably feel relieved to finally have an explanation for the curious behaviors you've been seeing in your child and to know that these behaviors are unintentional on the part of your child. Even though the signs have always been there, finally having a label for your child's predicament becomes both helpful and hurtful.

You will invariably go through a period of grieving, as you face the fact that your child has a neurological syndrome that she can't be expected to simply outgrow. Since her underlying deficiencies aren't going to go away, you must come to terms with her condition. You may feel overwhelmed by the reality that the child you had once seen as highly capable, actually has a serious and debilitating neurological disorder. And, you may feel unsure of your own capacity to meet her extensive needs. Then, as it all gradually sinks in, you will find yourself garnering the strength you need to become your child's unrelenting advocate.

Parenting a child with NLD requires a different set of parenting skills than would normally be called upon. It will take extra time and determination on your part to meet your child's unique needs. Unless you understand and accept the etiology behind your child's symptomology, your

DEFINITION

etiology
source or origin of a syndrome or a disease

symptomology
individual characteristics of a syndrome or disease

interactions with your child can become counterproductive and, in some cases, destructive.

A child who is blind usually elicits patience, sympathy, and extra attention from her parents. Parents customarily accept the fact that a blind child will require more of their time in order to advance successfully towards adulthood. Rarely is a blind child criticized or reprimanded for behavior resulting from her failure to see. On the other hand, a child with NLD doesn't often automatically receive the patience, sympathy, and extra attention that she needs in order to advance successfully toward adulthood. She is constantly criticized, reprimanded, and inundated with negative feedback for behavior resulting from her incoordination, visual-spatial-organizational deficiencies and failure to comprehend nonverbal communication.

One parent related the following analogy to me:

> She has a seven-year-old daughter who requires daily injections of insulin for her diabetes. She also has a nine-year-old son with NLD. This mother confessed that she is never too tired or too busy to give her daughter her insulin shot when it's required. That's a priority that never gets overlooked in their household. This same mom admits to sometimes slacking on her responsibilities to her son with NLD. She knows that because of his NLD she needs to tell him everything, that he needs previews and advance preparation, and that everything he does will take him longer to complete than other children his age. Some days, however, she's just too tired or too busy to accommodate and assist him.

> It wasn't until she realized that she was accommodating her daughter every day, regardless of her other obligations, but that her son only received the necessary accommodations when it was convenient for her, that she began making a concerted effort to consistently provide the guidance, support, and intervention that her son with NLD needs.

How Parents Can Take Action

The most important value in the proper identification of NLD is that after your child's syndrome has been identified, you will know what you need to focus on and you can take positive strides in that direction. Demystification is the first step in the long and, at times, overwhelming process of accepting and helping your child. This process involves educating yourself about how NLD affects learning and behavior. Seek out publications, conferences, and professionals who can help you to get a handle on your child's unique needs (some resources and organizations are listed in the **Support and Resources** section on page 178).

Understanding your child's learning style will increase your sensitivity toward her and enhance your ability to help her deal with the world more competently. With your help, she will begin filling in the pages of her "manual for living" (a line at a time). Eventually, she will learn to face the confusing and novel circumstances which confront her with more confidence and ability.

Witnessing the struggles and suffering of a child with nonverbal learning disorders can be an excruciating experience for a parent. All parents have certain hopes and dreams for their children, almost from the moment of conception. Abandoning these fantasies when your child is diagnosed with NLD, and accepting the reality that your child has a severe neurological disorder, can be a long and painful process. You may have been clinging to the secret belief that your child would eventually outgrow her idiosyncratic tendencies and be just like everyone else.

In order to move on with your lives, the misconception that NLD will be outgrown must be cast aside and replaced with the knowledge that your child will always approach the world differently. Feelings of loss, hurt, disappointment, anger, and ambivalence are not uncommon. The fact that your child's syndrome is "invisible," and not readily recognized by others, can also make it more difficult for you to acknowledge that the problem exists. And, somewhere along the way, it is natural for parents to experience a tremendous amount of guilt. You may blame yourself for your child's plight and agonize over mistakes you made before you fully understood your child's condition.

You will remember that Keisha's parents, in Chapter 2, thought they could change her unwanted behaviors through punishment. They didn't understand that Keisha was doing her best to conform and that none of her digressions were deliberate. Like many other parents, they believed the initial explanations that school officials and their family counselor gave them. When Keisha was finally diagnosed with NLD, and the ramifications were explained to her parents, they became despondent over their previous actions and attitudes toward her.

Likewise, Katie's mother had thought she could get her daughter to lighten up by friendly teasing, which Katie was unable to comprehend. When Katie's NLD was explained to her mother, she felt devastated to learn that she had been unwittingly adding to her daughter's frustrations. You, too, have probably made a few mistakes along the way, but at the time you made them, you did so for all the right reasons. Instead of looking back at the errors you've made in the past, look forward.

And please, always keep in mind that NLD has a neurological basis and that you aren't responsible for your child's learning disorders. You may have heard one or more of these unflattering remarks:

- Your child's social ineptitude results from a lack of exposure to social situations.

    The Source for Nonverbal Learning Disorders

- Your child's lack of organizational skills results from a dysfunctional home life.
- Your child's plethora of "rude" comments to others results from a lack of discipline in the home.

Of course, none of those assertions are even remotely true. Unfortunately, you will probably have to suffer through countless insinuations that you are a poor parent throughout your child's development. Learn to turn a deaf ear. Nothing you did or didn't do caused your child's NLD. Put away your guilt and move on to helping your child. She needs you more than most!

The protective propensities of the NLD child's parents can go a long way toward compensating for the unrealistic demands of the outside world and toward neutralizing the vulnerabilities of your child. Increased parental sensitivity, a supportive extended family, and acting on your gut level intuition are all approaches that will help you figure out what is best for your child. Follow your instincts. Your knowledge and understanding of your child's strengths and weaknesses will guide you in responding to your child's needs. If you recognize the early adjustment problems of the nonverbal learning disabilities syndrome in your child (detailed in Chapter 2), these signs should alert you to the fact that she is functioning with a different set of competencies than her peers.

Parents as Therapy Partners

It is advantageous to attempt to create a caring, protective environment at home, where your child can learn to use compensatory techniques in a non-threatening surrounding. However, to try to protect your child from all adverse situations which arise will eventually prove counterproductive, too, because she will inevitably have to deal with these situations on her own, at some point in her life. Home is the place where you must directly teach the skills which will help your child function more effectively in the outside world. Direct instruction in handling conflicts, decision-making, problem solving, and social interaction, which most children learn intuitively without ever having to be specifically taught, will help build your child's confidence and her ability to function more competently in the world outside the home.

As the parents of a child with NLD, you are your child's primary therapists. You have 24-hour-a-day access to your child, and you know her better than anyone else; you love her, and she loves you. Weekly therapy sessions with a professional won't often produce the desired results if parents aren't included in the program, because the child with NLD doesn't automatically generalize and apply information. When intervention is left solely up to professionals with little or no follow-through at home, it is almost certain that the child will continue to flounder.

Effective intervention programs encourage parents to be co-therapists and stress the importance of the parents' daily role in providing the guidance, support and acceptance their child with NLD needs.

Byron P. Rourke emphasizes the need for parent education in any integrated and comprehensive intervention program for the child with NLD:

> "One of the first steps in a remediation-habilitation program involves providing the parents with appropriate information concerning the nature and significance of their child's neuropsychological disabilities."

Parenting classes have proven helpful in instructing and supporting the parents of children with NLD in their efforts "to gear their expectations and their parenting methods and techniques" toward providing optimally for their children's unique needs. Dr. Rourke has found it "advisable and [in some cases] necessary to employ highly structured 'parenting' programs" for the parents of children with NLD.

A child grows and develops in two basic environments — home and school. If one of these environments fails her, it is crucial that the other one does not. Currently, the child with NLD doesn't automatically receive the recognition and accommodations she needs and is entitled to in the school environment. She is at an increased risk for being picked on by unenlightened peers and school staff. But if she receives understanding, assistance, and love from her parents and other family members, it can lessen the effects of any abusive behavior she may suffer at school. Parents must advocate unceasingly for the needs of a child with NLD. If you are a parent, you are the only constant factor in your child's life. She counts on you. No one else has the same level of commitment to your child that you do. And it is unlikely that her needs will be met without your direct involvement in the process.

Chances are your child doesn't experience the same degree of ineptitude at home as she does when confronting the outside world. This is because at home you are accustomed to your child's individual way of doing things and her specific competencies and incompetencies. Intuitively, you are probably serving a number of her unspoken needs. You may have already learned that:

- You have to explain everything to your child.
- Your child needs more help to master simple physical tasks.
- Daily routines should be kept the same.
- You must avoid surprises.

Special Challenges Parents Face

There is no doubt that an uncommon degree of stamina is required to parent a child with NLD. Interacting with this child calls for continuous pre-planning, constant vigilance, and a comprehensive understanding of the symptomology which results from a lack of access to the functions of the right hemisphere. At times, the challenges a parent of a child with NLD faces may appear overwhelming. Byron P. Rourke notes that "much extra time (as compared to that required for 'normal' children) is needed for interacting with [a child with NLD]. This is occasioned by their needs for repetition, practice, and step-by step monitoring when engaged in novel tasks."

In addition to increased alertness and deliberate forethought on your part, you must also be on the lookout at home for signs of depression in your child with NLD. Current medical theories suggest that undue stress causes depression. The child with NLD, because she doesn't adapt and apply past learning, enters every situation as a new challenge, and naturally encounters more stress in day-to-day living than her peers. Like Katie, she will probably have difficulty adjusting to changes, worry excessively, fear new situations, and be constantly confused by the ease with which others seem to glide through life.

Your child may end up blaming herself for her failures, casting additional criticism upon herself and believing that no matter how hard she tries, her actions will all prove futile. Due to her lack of access to her right hemisphere functions, every aspect of her day will be more stressful for her than for others, leaving her extremely vulnerable to developing depression. Keep in mind that, although NLD is a neurological impairment and, as such, cannot be "cured," the depression which results from NLD can be successfully treated by medical professionals familiar with NLD.

Strategies for Parenting the Child with NLD

Basic proficiencies for parenting a child with NLD can be broken down as follows. (A summary sheet of this information in included on pages 67-68.)

1. **Recognize the neurological basis of NLD.** The first step in increasing your proficiency as the parent of a child with non-verbal learning disabilities is to understand and accept the etiology of NLD. Having an explanation for the unusual behaviors and inconsistent abilities you've been observing equips you to better deal with your own frustrations, as well as the unkind comments of others. Knowledge empowers you to develop the skills you need to help your child. For some parents, gaining a basic understanding of the syndrome affecting their child can change

their whole relationship with that child. All of the interventions detailed in this book will prove more effective, if you truly perceive *why* they should be implemented, and not just that they *should* be implemented.

2. **Educate yourself regarding the symptomology which results from a lack of access to the processes of the right hemisphere.** It is important to have realistic expectations of your child's capabilities. Studies have shown that most parents overestimate the competency of their child with NLD. Acquiring a better perspective of the specific areas of development which are impacted by NLD prepares you to react with compassion when your child is struggling. Parents need to be able to make a distinction between incompetence and noncompliance.

   The child with NLD, by virtue of her disorder, is generally more compliant than most other children. Eventually, practically all parents come to realize that the behavioral problems their child with NLD experiences result from incompetence, rather than noncompliance. Because she sees everything as black or white — good or bad (with no gray areas), the child with NLD is less likely than her peers to knowingly engage in behavior which is not acceptable. This child doesn't make excuses for her behavior and readily admits, "Yes, I did that." This is because, at the time she did it, she saw nothing wrong with it.

   "Ignorance is no excuse," but in the case of a youngster with NLD, a wide latitude must be allowed for her lack of competencies. Her motoric deficiencies, visual-spatial-organizational limitations, and social blunders should be dealt with through accommodation and skill building, never punishment. Punishing a child with NLD who appears noncompliant, is the same as punishing a child who is blind for bumping into something she didn't see. Instead, one would hope you would assist the blind child by providing her with a cane or some other compensatory modification to help her adjust to a world designed for those with vision.

   The incompetencies of a child with NLD must not be viewed as "behavior to change," but rather as limitations to be supported and accommodated in an alternate fashion. Punishment and fear will only make your child more anxious, more nervous, and more likely to "mess up." Punishing a child may stop the behavior, but it won't teach a more appropriate strategy to your child. Punishment will actually hurt the performance of the child. Instead of resorting to punishment, provide your child with compensatory modifications to help her adjust to a world designed for those with fully functioning right hemisphere systems.

62   *The Source for Nonverbal Learning Disorders*

3. **Verbally teach your child the things that other children learn intuitively or through observation.** She learns best when taught in a very deliberate fashion. While other children her age are discovering concepts and principles, your child needs to have everything pointed out to her. Effective intervention methods include direct verbal training in the following:

   - planning
   - discriminating
   - organizing
   - studying
   - temporal concepts
   - written expression
   - abstract reasoning
   - decision-making and problem solving
   - social cognition
   - interpersonal communication.

   Help your child get a verbal handle on the abstract concepts that confuse her. Use verbal indicators to enable your child to know what she should be doing. And, verbally explain your emotions to help your child read and understand you better:

   > **Example:** You may want to exaggerate your facial expressions and verbally label them for your child. You might say, "I'm getting really angry," as your face stiffens and turns red.

   Previews and rehearsals should precede any new situations. But remember, practice doesn't necessarily make perfect. We usually make the assumption that the more times someone repeats an action, the easier and more automatic it becomes. We expect that the child will apply this new learning to similar situations. A "learning through reppetition" approach doesn't work for the child with NLD because she doesn't acclimatize through repetition.

4. **Provide as safe an environment as possible for your child within your home.** Don't forget that your child's motor coordination and spatial reference lag behind that of her peers. When your child is young, it is advisable to remove any dangerous obstacles from your living areas. Develop a safe, soft play area using a spare mattress or large cushions on the floor where your child can practice balancing skills without too much danger of injury. This also creates a nice, soft play space where your child can sprawl out with her toys. Supervise your child's free-time activities long after you think such supervision should be necessary.

5. **Provide as secure an environment as possible for your child within your home.** If your child feels threatened or scared, she will either act out or withdraw. Instead of punishing her for behaviors you find incongruent, offer her a hug and try to figure out why she is feeling insecure. Interact calmly and positively with your child with NLD. This child carries the risk of eventually perceiving her situation as hopeless, which can result in serious internalizing psychopathology, such as depression, withdrawal, anxiety, and panic attacks. As parents, you must strive to reduce the negative feedback your child receives from her environment, to ward off the harbingers of these frightening secondary outcomes. Don't insist your child take on more than she is ready to handle, even if you feel she *should* be able to do the things you ask. As was mentioned before, always be alert for signs of depression in your child with NLD.

6. **Provide consistent schedules and constructive routines.** Predictability within the home will help ease some of the stress your child experiences throughout the day.

   Example: The night before school, help your child select and line up the clothes she will wear the next day. Setting them out in the order she will put them on is helpful. The child with NLD may establish the habit of counting the items because it is easier for her to remember rote information, as opposed to visual information.

   The number and sequence are important to her. She may only be able to determine she's dressed when she has put on six items, rather than by looking in the mirror and discerning visually that she is fully clothed. Eventually your child will learn to go through this routine on her own, but dressing will always require some advance planning for her — this isn't an adult who can pull something out of the closet at the last minute, throw it on, and rush out the door (or she may end up at work in her bathrobe!). Consciously strive to establish sequential routines within your home that your child can ultimately carry out on her own. The goal is the attainment of self-sufficiency in a predictable, non-threatening environment.

   Daily expectations should be explained in careful, sequential detail. Provide written lists for your child that divide tasks into their component parts. The child with NLD doesn't visualize, so she will have difficulty remembering a series of directions. Instead of asking your child to "Get dressed and come to breakfast," make a list for her in the order the activities should be performed.

The Source for Nonverbal Learning Disorders

Getting Dressed
- Wash your face and hands.
- Brush your teeth.
- Comb your hair.
- Put on the clean clothes that you laid out last night.
- Now come to eat your breakfast.

Or, instead of asking your child to "Clean your room," again, you need to break it down into components:

Cleaning Your Bedroom
- Make your bed.
- Put the clothes that need to be washed into the hamper.
- Pick up your toys and put them on the shelf.
- Dust your furniture.
- Vacuum the carpet.

Obviously, these lists will expand as the child gets older. However, the need to define the details of specifically what has to be done to accomplish something will remain. Always be specific about what you expect. Your requests should be reasonable and suited to your child's capabilities. Be careful not to overload her, as this child is easily overwhelmed.

7. **Take the time to explain changes in routine before they happen, so that your child can prepare for what is to come next.** If your child is involved in an activity, don't suddenly insist that she stop. Give her several verbal warnings so she has time to achieve some closure and can transition more smoothly to the next activity. Insecurity results from encountering unknown territory. Your child will feel less anxious about changes and novel situations if she is prepared for them beforehand. Don't assume she will adapt naturally, in the way most children do.

    Try not to introduce too many new things at once. Your child needs time to test the water with her toes before she puts her whole foot in. Don't suddenly leave her on her own. Instead, slowly fade out of the picture, providing her with the support she needs, for as long as she needs it. The child with NLD is very slow to adapt to new input and new situations. Be sure she has been given an adequate amount of time to assimilate the old, before introducing any new expectations.

Adult authority figures should strive not to be too rigid, too bossy, or too abrupt when dealing with the child with NLD. Encourage your child's efforts to do things for herself, but don't expect too much too soon. Her timetable will be different from that of her peers. Look for small steps of progress, not huge leaps.

8. **A proactive approach is always preferable to a reactive approach.** Your goal should be to anticipate and prepare ahead for obstacles your child is likely to encounter, owing to NLD. Offer simple explanations of what is happening at all times. Sometimes you will need to manipulate the environment in order to reduce the likelihood of a difficult social situation for your child. Early on, limit play sessions to one, and then two, children at any one time. You will also need to keep a close watch out that your child is not being taken advantage of by others. As a parent, you should continuously evaluate the effectiveness of your efforts and adjust your future plans accordingly.

9. **Any outside therapy your child receives must be followed up at home.** An hour or so of outside intervention per week (be it educational, occupational, speech and language, and/or counseling therapy) will have no lasting effect unless you continue and reinforce the techniques in your home. Remember, as parents, you are your child's primary therapists.

10. **Don't forget to have fun with your child with NLD.** Conduct an inventory of the many assets your child has. Be sure you take time to appreciate her remarkable gifts as you strive to help her to work around her areas of deficit. Incorporate time into your schedule to encourage and explore together her areas of special interest and her own particular talents. As you and your child have fun together, the world will become a less threatening place for your child.

You have been entrusted with the care of a unique and wonderful individual who has a lot to offer the world. Acknowledge her on a regular basis, just because she is your child and you love her. Be careful not to spend all your time focusing on her areas of difficulty. Enjoy your time with her! You need to ensure that she experiences some sunshine in a world which can appear very dark most of the time.

66 *The Source for Nonverbal Learning Disorders*

Summary of Reminders and Strategies
For Parents of Children with NLD

1. **Recognize the neurological basis of NLD.**
   - Having an explanation for your child's behaviors and inconsistent abilities equips you to better deal with your frustrations as they arise.
   - The techniques you use with your child will be more effective if you understand *why* they are necessary.

2. **Educate yourself about the symptomatology which results from a lack of access to the processes of the right hemisphere.**
   - NLD is a neurological problem, not a behavioral problem.
   - Punishing a child with NLD for inappropriate behavior is futile, since the child is unable to interpret social situations correctly and will not learn from your punishment.

3. **Verbally teach your child the things that other children learn intuitively or through observation.**
   - Teach your child in a verbal and very direct manner.
   - Preview and rehearse new situations (a party, first day of school, etc.).
   - Don't assume that repetitive practice and rehearsal will result in learning or adaptation.

4. **Provide as physically safe an environment as possible for your child within your home.**
   - Your child's motor coordination lags behind his peers.
   - Remove dangerous obstacles from living areas.
   - Use a spare mattress or large cushions to create a soft play area on the floor.

5. **Provide as emotionally secure an environment as possible for your child within your home.**
   - If your child begins to feel threatened or scared, she will either act out or withdraw.
   - Instead of punishing your child for acting out, offer a hug and try to find the root of her insecurity.
   - A positive home environment will help offset the negative experiences your child faces in the outside world.

6. **Provide a consistent schedule and constructive routines within your home.**

   - Consistency at home will ease some of the stress your child experiences throughout the day.

   - Provide written lists that divide household tasks (getting dressed, cleaning bedroom) into component parts.

7. **Explain changes in routine before they happen to prepare your child for what is to come next.**

   - Do not insist your child stop a task he is involved in immediately; instead, provide several verbal warnings to allow him to achieve closure.

   - Do not introduce too many new things at once.

   - Provide support and slowly "fade out of the picture" in a novel situation, rather than expecting your child to approach it independently.

   - Be flexible, rather than rigid or bossy; encourage independence but don't expect too much too soon.

8. **Be proactive rather than reactive.**

   - Anticipate potential obstacles and prepare your child to meet them.

   - Be prepared to manipulate the environment to reduce the likelihood of a difficult social situation for your child (for example, limiting the number of playmates).

9. **Follow up outside therapy at home.**

   - An hour of outside intervention every week will be ineffective unless you follow through at home.

   - Remember, you must be your child's primary therapist.

10. **Don't forget to have fun together.**

   - Make note of all the positive characteristics of your child.

   - Appreciate your child's gifts as you work around her areas of difficulty.

   - Have fun spending time together; this will help make the world a less threatening place for your child.

Chapter 6

Accommodating a Child's Nonverbal Learning Disorders at School

Even when a child has been correctly diagnosed with NLD, it may still be difficult for him to receive the program modifications and accommodations he needs in school . . .

In 1985, Adam transferred from a New Jersey school district and was placed in my Resource Specialist Program in a California school district. He brought with him an IEP specifying the handicapping condition of NLD. At that time, I had been working in various special education programs in California for nearly 15 years, had specialist credentials in the areas of learning and behavior, had received my Master's in Special Education in 1981, and had never heard of the term *nonverbal learning disabilities syndrome*.

I consulted with a school psychologist, who fortunately was then working on his doctorate, and seemed to be vaguely familiar with NLD. He explained to me that Adam was very bright, but had a significant discrepancy between his (high) verbal IQ and (low) performance IQ. I was told that this produced difficulties for him in the area of writing. I was also apprised that we didn't generally "offer special education services to such children in California." Since Adam had an existing IEP, I was advised to work with him for 30 days, during which time we would reassess him to determine what type of services he qualified for in our district.

I immediately sought information about NLD and, with difficulty, eventually located a few sources in a hospital medical library. But when I first met Adam, any understanding I thought I had about his disorder went flying out the door, as he waltzed in. A bouncy third-grader with pudgy cheeks hidden in a mass of overlapping freckles, he instantly made his presence known to all. Even though I knew his strengths were in verbal skills, I was surprised when he walked in my classroom jabbering and never stopped. Somehow, I had expected him to be nonverbal. Adam was anything but! And it didn't take long to discern that he had an excellent vocabulary for his age.

Adam had only been in my program a few weeks when I attended a Cub Scout meeting where he gave a short speech. Nine-year-old Adam used words like *majestic* and *effervescent* to describe the mountains and the lake he had encountered on a recent camping trip. I heard the other adults around me whispering, "It's obvious someone else told him what to say." I knew those were Adam's words, because I knew Adam. If you weren't familiar with Adam, though, his oration did sound phoney and a bit pedantic, because no one expects a small child to speak like an eloquent adult.

Adam had already been given some computer keyboarding instruction at his previous school in New Jersey. He wrote well, but it took him forever to get his thoughts on paper, even with a word processor. In addition, his regular classroom teacher complained to me constantly about his non-stop talking and other "annoying" behaviors. Members of the school assessment team suggested that Adam must have ADD, because he didn't seem to censor his speech and was often out of his seat, wandering around.

Adam's parents were clearly looking for answers and were open to suggestions, but they rejected a suggestion from our school psychologist that they approach Adam's pediatrician about the possibility of a trial period on medication. Medication had already been tried, they related. When Adam was younger, prior to his NLD diagnosis, he had been diagnosed with ADD and put on Ritalin. It was discontinued within a short time, when Adam developed headaches, dizziness, and incontinence.

I know his parents must have felt let down by the lack of servicing then available for NLD students in California. The following year Adam's family moved back to New Jersey. Ten years later, there is definitely more information available about NLD (Byron Rourke's first complete book on the subject was published in 1989 and a second came out in 1995), but it doesn't appear that the attitudes and awareness levels of most professionals about NLD have changed much.

Availability of Services for Children with NLD

In California, the level of service and responsibility assumed by state and local agencies in addressing the needs of students with NLD in our public schools varies widely. I believe it is fair to say that, at this point in time, *most students with NLD today aren't receiving adequate services, and therefore, aren't receiving a free appropriate public education, as PL 94-142 requires.* Our existing school system tends to discriminate unfairly against the child with nonverbal learning disorders. As it currently stands, parents are often forced to enlist outside professionals to help them demand their child's right to a free appropriate public education. Various advocacy organizations, including the following, are currently researching the rights of the child with NLD to receive special education services:

- Community Alliance for Special Education (CASE)
- Protection and Advocacy, Inc. (PAI)
- Disability Rights Education and Defense Fund (DREDF)
- the Learning Disabilities Association of America (LDA)
- SHARE Support, Inc.

To date, no legislation has been enacted specifically to address the needs of children with NLD.

The child with NLD most appropriately qualifies for special education services under the category of Other Health Impaired (OHI), a category used to define the services needed for students with neurologic and physical impairments, as well as chronic health problems, including these:

- cerebral palsy
- muscular sclerosis
- AD/HD
- epilepsy
- severe asthma
- cystic fibrosis

Why NLD is Considered a Learning Disability

All learning requires both verbal and nonverbal processes. The child with NLD is considered learning disabled for the following reasons:

- New learning (especially in complex or novel situations) is difficult.
- He overrelies on previously learned rote information.
- His deficiencies in adaptability naturally produce deficiencies in learning.
- His information processing capacities are limited to unimodal processing (as opposed to intermodal integration) of information.

Invariably, extensive interventions will need to be provided to guarantee appropriate treatment of a child with NLD in school. NLD is a chronic neurological/medical condition which results in obstruction to adaptive learning (leading to social and vocational incompetencies), and thereby significantly and adversely affects the student's educational performance. Special education support and services are needed in order to ensure this student the right to an appropriate educational opportunity that meets his unique needs.

Nonverbal learning disorders also currently fit the definition of a low incidence disability. Low incidence disability means a severe disabling condition with an expected incidence rate of less than one percent of the total statewide enrollment for kindergarten through grade 12. As such, public school districts are required to ensure that "regular and special education staff are adequately prepared to provide educational instruction and services to these individuals" and that "the assessment of a pupil with a suspected low incidence disability shall be conducted by persons knowledgeable of that disability."

Educating Educators About NLD

There may be only a handful of students at any given school, at any given time, with NLD. Because of this low rate of incidence, few educators have a working knowledge of nonverbal learning disorders. When shool staff encounter this child, most are ill-prepared to meet his educational or social needs. Teachers and other school personnel need to be trained to spot the early adjustment problems seen in a student with nonverbal learning disabilities syndrome and be better equipped to implement appropriate CAMS (compensations, accommodations, modifications, and strategies) for this student. Only then can the child with NLD be treated with the competence and justice he deserves.

Teachers should be aware of the behaviors interfering with classroom performance which may be indicative of a non-language-based learning disability. It is important to remember that not all of these characteristics will be present in every child with NLD. Nonetheless, the following observations should alert a teacher that a student may have some sort of neurologically-based nonverbal learning deficit:

1. The left margin of written work tends to slope to the right and to become progressively wider as the student's writing moves down the page (especially if there is no left margin line provided on the paper).

2. Multi-step directions may be confused or forgotten because this student can't visualize to support auditory input.

3. Diagonals (especially left sloping) are difficult for this student to perceive. This makes both manuscript and cursive writing frustrating and laborious to master.

4. This student will have difficulty gaining meaningful information from visual displays, such as charts, graphs, mobiles, maps, diagrams, clock faces, etc. He will also experience distress attempting to duplicate (copy) visual-spatial material.

5. Plane integration is often disturbed. This student may experience great difficulty copying at his desk (horizontal plane) from the blackboard (vertical plane). Tracking difficulties, irregular eye pursuits, midline eye jerk and visual-spatial-organizational deficits also make the copying of assignments disorganized and tedious.

6. This student will probably have excellent rote memory skills, but the visual-spatial alignment of numbers can make basic math skills difficult to master.

7. This student spells phonetically. Errors in spelling tend to be close phonetic approximations (*b-i-n* for *b-e-e-n*), easily identified with the actual word desired (vowels are often omitted). Written spelling is more difficult for this student than oral spelling. Nonphonetic words will prove problematic because the most effective way to memorize this type of word is to visualize the word, and this technique is unavailable to the student with NLD.

Learning involving primarily left-hemisphere functions won't generally present a problem for the student with NLD. Expect this student to excel in the following:

- reading
- spelling
- vocabulary
- memorization of rote facts

The following academic tasks involving right-hemisphere functions can be difficult to impossible:

- organizational skills
- study skills
- written expression
- comprehension
- temporal concepts
- discrimination of attributes
- body image
- abstract reasoning
- problem solving
- social cognition
- interpersonal communication

The young student with NLD usually doesn't receive any services in elementary school because his deficits in right hemisphere functions have not yet created a significant impact upon his school performance. This is a travesty because all current research strongly indicates that *early intervention* is imperative to ensure the continued success of this student throughout his schooling. Referrals to the Student Study Team at school are typically generated by the student's failure to complete written assignments in upper elementary or middle school. Prior to such a referral, this student may have exhibited a number of behavioral concerns which were probably not properly identified with his neurological syndrome.

Inclusion and the Student with NLD

Inclusive schooling is ordinarily the best option for all students and the student with NLD is no exception. Within a well-developed inclusion program, the CAMS utilized to benefit the student with NLD will also benefit other mainstreamed students as well. Below are some of the arguments for inclusion:

- Inclusive schooling helps create a society in which individual differences are better tolerated, accepted and accommodated, rather than shunted and ignored.

- Programs which integrate children with and without disabilities naturally promote the development of understanding and acceptance.

- It is important that all students have the opportunity to shape their attitudes towards human differences by practical example during their school years.

- The positive attitudes which develop as a result of accepting human differences at a young age will hopefully carry on into these students' adult lives, and they will have gained the skills and empathy needed to deal compassionately with employees, customers, clients, neighbors, friends, or mates with individual differences and challenges.

- Segregation of students who require accommodation is a poor substitute for well-integrated educational programs.

The following characteristics of a child with NLD generally support full inclusion as the most appropriate setting for learning:

- a typically high level of intelligence
- a propensity to profit from group interaction and discussion
- behavioral inconsistencies which almost always improve with understanding and appropriate servicing

Unfortunately, though, the resistive attitudes of some teachers, and their steadfast refusal to implement appropriate accommodations for the child with NLD, will often cause full inclusion to prove less than desirable. However, there is no sound educational reason why the majority of students with NLD can't be successfully educated in regular classrooms, if the staff involved approach their responsibilities with a willingness to try a different approach and an open attitude toward change.

Attempts at full inclusion may also prove to be unsuccessful if the student with NLD is placed into multiple classrooms with teachers whose styles and philosophies vary widely. Remember, this child has difficulties with adaptability. He will probably not adjust well to the differing expectations of a diverse staff. It is always preferable to limit the number of adults this student must deal with on a daily basis. When a student is

74 *The Source for Nonverbal Learning Disorders*

placed in multiple classrooms, it is also difficult for his case manager to sufficiently communicate with all of his teachers and to ensure that necessary CAMS are provided on a consistent and ongoing basis. The fewer people involved in the program, the more efficient the program becomes. Communication and collaboration between staff members, and between the educational staff and the child's parents are the principal determinants of a successful inclusion program.

Some Strategies for Successful Inclusion

Following are some tips for working in the classroom with a student with NLD.

1. **Minimize the number of adults assigned to work with this student.** All staff involved should be made aware that they will need to consult and plan together frequently in order to provide a consistent intervention program for the student with NLD. Successful intervention requires that staff members communicate and collaborate daily.

2. **Analyze the student's strengths and interests.** His strong verbal skills should be used as a primary means for acquiring additional skills. The future successes of this child are dependent upon his acquisition of compensatory strategies, usually verbal, to circumvent his areas of incompetency. This student learns primarily through discussion. Don't make the mistake of isolating him from other students.

3. **Monitor the student's organizational skills daily.** An assignment notebook will help him to keep organized and can also be used for discreet individualization. The teacher should assume responsibility for updating the notebook — not the student with NLD.

4. **Define processes in a linear, sequential format that can be memorized verbally.** You might explain a writing assignment by saying, "An expository paragraph should have five sentences: an opening sentence, three supporting sentences, and a concluding sentence." (Since this student doesn't visualize, don't ask him to think of a paragraph as a "hamburger" — this type of visualization strategy will only confuse his literal, logical way of thinking and slow the retention process for him.) The student with NLD loves clearly defined, numbered rules.

Most children automatically observe patterns and relation-ships; they spontaneously discover meaning and intent without realizing they are actually learning in the process. No attempt is made at memorization; instead, the typical child integrates his concrete experiences and then forms cor-responding concepts and principals. In contrast, the child with NLD starts by memorizing rote verbal information and acquires a tremendous store of general knowledge through his accumulated verbal interpretation. Don't expect discovery learning from this child. Because he doesn't discover patterns and relationships, the child with NLD needs verbal explana-tions and guided sequential demonstrations. He *will* learn — the process is just different for him than for most of his class-mates.

5. **Monitor and adjust assignments on a daily basis.** Use alternate testing procedures as needed. Timed assignments only produce stress — eliminate them. Allow the student to experience closure. Because he processes slowly and has diffi-culty with transitions, it is better to let him complete one assignment, than to only do portions of several assignments.

6. **Provide the student with NLD enough support to expe-rience success with the regular classroom curriculum.** This support is intended to level the playing field and to enable this student to fulfill his teacher's academic goals and requirements (without the expectancy that he must complete every assignment dispensed). Previewing and supplemental aids (such as study guides, outlines, and audiocassettes of the material to be covered in class) will allow this student to receive the maximum benefit from the classroom instruction which comes afterwards.

7. **Do not allow your grading system to discriminate against the student with NLD.** You will defeat your own objectives if you base grades merely upon the number of assignments completed. This quantitative type of grading system places an unfair disadvantage upon the student with visual-spatial-organizational deficits, who may in fact be learning more and working harder than the other students in your class, but who simply can't complete the same number of assignments. Using the number of completed assignments as a grading criteria (with points lost for incomplete assign-ments) penalizes the student for his neurological condition and doesn't take into account his actual effort, progress, and learning.

8. **Be positive.** A positive attitude toward the student, an enthusiasm for teaching, a sense of humor, and a willingness to make changes and adjustments in programs are the key components needed for a successful staff working with the student with NLD.

Developing an Inclusion Plan

Special education is a series of individually designed services and supports; it is not a place to which a student is assigned. A child is not either "in" or "out" of special education; his intervention plan should be in effect in every class he attends, during every passing period, during recesses and breaks, on every field trip, and at every assembly. Since each student is unique, the student's IEP provides the individual framework for appropriate CAMS, which should be implemented *throughout the school day*. Successful implementation of an inclusionary placement requires careful planning. Regular education and special education personnel must plan together for the educational and social integration needs of a student with NLD. Open communication between parents and school staff is also imperative.

Ideally, the inclusion program for the upcoming school year should be developed and set up during the spring prior to the coming school year. The planning and implementation phase can be decisive, yet frequently little time is devoted to this stage of the process. Compensations, accommodations, modifications, and strategies should be clearly defined and put into place from day one of the school year. All educators must be ready and willing to implement changes in the way they've always done things, in order for an intervention plan to prove successful for a child. Proper implementation doesn't just happen because a good plan is in place; it also takes a high level of professional commitment from the school staff. Inservice training *must* be provided for all faculty members involved with this student. The child with NLD requires *daily* modifications of assignments and *consistent* accommodations for his areas of disability. Careful planning is crucial to forming a successful program and *communication* is the key to keeping it running smoothly.

To develop effective teaching strategies, it is important to differentiate NLD from other learning disorders. As we have seen, specific intervention techniques will be different from those employed for other subtypes of learning disabilities or those employed for behavioral or emotional disorders. Although the child with NLD learns differently from his peers, he learns rote material quickly and easily. He seems to have endless storage space in his memory and he constantly absorbs details and information. Capitalize on these strengths. His strong verbal skills should be used as a primary means for acquiring additional skills. The future successes of this child are dependent upon his acquisition of compensatory strategies, usually verbal, to circumvent his areas of incompetency.

Teacher lesson plans must take into account the fact that a student with NLD has difficulty processing information presented primarily through the visual modality. Keep the following in mind when dealing with presentation of information:

- Take visual overkill out of worksheets.
- Supplement visually-presented materials with verbal input.
- Written responses should not be the exclusive method of evaluating the child's learning. Always determine the goal of the task. Don't torture a child needlessly who has difficulty with handwriting when an oral response could be substituted in place of a written response.
- Leave enough response space on worksheets to allow for poor graphomotor control.

The CAMS recommended for the individual with NLD are all relatively inexpensive to develop and implement. Following are some guidelines for the presentation of material, as well as suggestions for modifications in each of the major curricular areas.

Reading

Learning to Read
The student with NLD will probably be one of the top readers in his class. Learning to read is dependent upon verbal memory reception, verbal memory retrieval, and verbal memory expression — all processes of the left-hemisphere. This student should excel in reading programs which apply a guided, sequential, phonetic/linguistic approach to reading rather than a more holistic whole language/sight reading approach. Auditory cues will help this child learn new words; don't rely on flash cards, Rebus sentences, picture-words or other predominantly visual methods.

Do Not Hold This Student Back
A sequential approach is important, but make sure the student is allowed to move forward quickly once the required material is learned. Too much repetition is frustrating for a mind that easily memorizes new verbal information. Remember that this child's word recognition skills are already likely to be far beyond those of his peers. Let him move on to the next level as soon as he is ready. Chances are this student already taught himself to read before entering school (a large number of children with NLD do).

Previewing Material
In the upper grades, be sure to provide this student with outlines and notes of any material to be read ahead of time, so that he can preview and prepare. Allow him to use a highlighting marker to highlight these notes while the other students are taking notes

from their reading. Or, have the special education department purchase consumable reading texts for this student, so that he can highlight important information right in the book.

Comprehension Concerns

Remember, comprehension difficulties will arise from hidden meanings. The student with NLD probably won't experience any problem remembering the specific details of what he has read, but he will have trouble making inferences. Comprehension for context at the literal level should be fine. This student is able to analyze the information, but he can't evaluate it. Teach and stress reading comprehension. Step-by-step guidance will be needed to help this student formulate answers to questions which are open-ended ("Why do you suppose she did that?" or "What could he have done differently?"). This student will not "read between the lines."

Reading Time

Although this student probably reads quite well for his age, he will still need extra time to complete reading assignments because of his slow processing rate and because of his visual-spatial difficulties. Do not require long stretches of continuous reading, because this can result in visual fatigue for the child with NLD. Having to attend visually for long periods can lead to eye strain and a loss of concentration. Watch for signs of eye strain while the student is reading:

- red eyes
- rubbing and blinking of the eyes
- squinting
- laying his head on the desk
- complaints of headaches

Do not assign catch-up reading as homework. Strive to minimize the number and length of reading assignments requiring long periods of visual concentration.

Written Language

The Demands of Writing

Written language involves a multitude of skills, calling on both right and left hemisphere functions. The student with NLD almost always struggles with the process of writing. This is partly because he has to concentrate so hard on the actual mechanics of handwriting that he "forgets" or is unable to formulate what he wants to write, and partly because he experiences great difficulty trying to transfer his ideas from his brain onto his paper in a written format. NLD is known to cause problems putting thoughts in writing.

An incapacity to cross information between the left and right hemispheres of the brain contributes to difficulty putting creative thoughts (right hemisphere) into writing (left hemisphere). The student with NLD doesn't visualize and therefore can't keep a story line going in his head. An inability to sift through too many details stored in his memory can also impede the writing process for this child.

All of these factors result in the student having inadequate resources to even begin a typical, grade-appropriate writing assignment. He may sit for long periods of time staring at his paper, unable to actually proceed. The crossover from understanding to doing is laborious. It may take him 10 minutes just to put his pencil to his paper.

Break Down Assignments
It is imperative that teachers break down all written assignments and reports into their smallest possible component parts. Give the student with NLD specific instructions for the assignment, in bite-size increments (as opposed to all at once). Start with factual writing before expecting more imaginative, creative efforts. Let the student pick a topic of interest to him. This child is likely to produce written composition in a random order, because he focuses on the details and not the complete work. Once he has generated an idea, assist him in creating an outline to follow. Gradually work toward decreasing the amount of structure you need to provide, as the student becomes more proficient and more confident in his ability to write.

Assist in Organization
When assigning research papers, this student will need to have the steps presented to him one at a time, initially. He is unable to break down the ultimate goal into its sectional goals. If you assign a large project, this student will not be able to separate the outcome of that project into its pieces in order to arrive at his finished product. He can't coordinate the segments that he has completed to put it all together at the end. Guide him on to the next phase only after the previous stage has been completed. An introductory overview of an entire project may prove to be too overwhelming, causing this child to shut down completely.

Reward Quality Over Quantity

Always look at the quality of a completed written assignment, rather than the quantity produced. One quality paragraph can substitute for several paragraphs. Remember to keep your goals in mind. If the goal of the assignment is not written language, allow the student to demonstrate his knowledge in an alternate format. Capitalize on his strengths. An oral presentation may suffice in place of a written report. Once the obstacle of writing is removed, this student will really be able to show you what he knows.

Interpret Behavior Correctly

Failure of the student to get started or even to be able to start a writing assignment must not be viewed as disobedience. The student may say "I'm not doing this," but he is not being rebellious. He is letting you know he *can't* do it, yet.

Electronic Assistance

And last, but not least, provide the student with NLD with a word processor or laptop computer to use on all written assignments of any length. Don't let his dysgraphia get in the way of his ability to communicate in writing.

Spelling

Strengths and Weaknesses

The student with NLD is generally an excellent speller. Any spelling errors are usually phonetically accurate and the misspelled words are easily recognizable. Omission or misplacement of vowels are the most common spelling mistakes (who needs them, anyway?) made by the child with NLD. Keeping in mind his superior aptitude for spelling, there are also specific difficulties which should be kept in mind when planning an approach to spelling curriculum.

Decrease Emphasis on Visual Approach

Don't ask this child to copy his spelling words from the board or to write them 10 times each. He doesn't learn visually and shouldn't be asked to copy material in this manner. When copying is absolutely necessary, be sure to provide a close-up model for the child to copy from. It is preferable to eliminate copying assignments for this student. And remember, repetitious writing will not reinforce his knowledge of a word's spelling. This becomes an exercise in finger dexterity for him, not a reinforcement of spelling words. Don't present too many new words at once; this can be visually overwhelming for the child with NLD.

Emphasize Auditory Strategies

The student with NLD may need parallel activities to practice spelling because he is predominantly an auditory learner. As with every subject, the most effective methods for him will be ones that capitalize on his verbal strengths. Words presented visually should always be supplemented with auditory prompting. Be careful not to rely on visually confusing spelling reinforcement exercises, such as spelling Bingo and word hunts.

Rhymes and songs can be taught to help this student remember the correct sequence of letters. Instead of paper and pencil tasks, let him practice his spelling words orally (on tape). He can read the word and then repeat the letters out loud. Verbally point out silent letters. This emphasis will help him remember to include letters that he can't hear. Once the child knows how to spell a word, excessive repetition is not necessary. Allow him to move on.

Spelling Time As Success Time

It has been recommended by Dr. Rourke that spelling curriculum be replaced with extra physical education time for the student with NLD. Although spelling instruction may prove redundant, I say, at least, let this child take the spelling test with his class. Spelling is an area where he can excel and receive the admiration of his classmates. The student with NLD also does very well in oral spelling bees. Give him his chance to shine!

Mathematics

Visual-Spatial Problems

The visual-spatial nature of math activities can confuse the student with NLD. Problems arise in the following areas:

- spatial organization (aligning numbers in columns, perceiving directionality, and construing correct spacing)
- visual relationship (dollar signs, decimal points, etc., may be improperly placed)
- graphomotor deficiencies (a tendency to write large numbers produces crowding and disorientation)
- failure to generalize (a previously learned skill is not adapted to be used in a slightly different situation)

Problems are not usually seen in the areas of knowledge of facts or sequence of operations. Arithmetic facts are easily memorized and coded by the student with NLD.

82 *The Source for Nonverbal Learning Disorders*

Step-by-Step Approach

As with all subjects, a step-by-step, structured, sequential approach will work best in mathematics. Never assume that this child will automatically apply a previously learned concept to a new concept. Point out the similarities to him that other students discover on their own. The child with NLD needs as many concrete facts as you can give him because his abstract reasoning is deficient. Be sure to verbally describe each step of a problem as you demonstrate it; what you don't say will not be seen or understood. The words, "Now watch what I'm doing here . . ." must be replaced with a precise verbal explanation. Don't ask this student to study an example in the text before you have given him a detailed verbal description of the process being illustrated.

Move Beyond the Visual

Math instruction should not rely solely on drawings, diagrams, and other visual displays. When demonstrating a new concept, explain each step in its sequential order verbally to the student. Ask him to verbalize each step back to you while he is practicing the procedure. If you listen to the child as he verbalizes the problem, you will be able to know whether or not he has grasped the concept you are teaching. Don't rely on his written responses, which may only represent his visual-spatial difficulties.

Remember, visual manipulatives may add to this child's visual-spatial confusion, while at the same time accentuating his poor planning abilities and fine-motor difficulties. Unifix cubes are probably the best of the currently available manipulatives because they snap together. Not only are they less likely to move around once they've been put into place, but the student will also receive an extra auditory cue from the snapping sound they make.

Reduce Visual Distractions

Math texts that rely upon lots of color and pictures can overwhelm the student with NLD. A simple layout with black and white text will be less visually confusing. Also *not* recommended are texts which jump back and forth between concepts. This child needs a consistent, sequential presentation. As in other subjects, allow him to move forward quickly once a concept is mastered.

Use a Consumable Text

It is always preferable to have the special education department purchase a consumable math text for the student with NLD. This eliminates the student having to copy the problems onto another sheet of paper. He will be able to spend more time on his calculations and be better able to show you what he has learned. If consumable texts aren't available, and the student's text can't be marked in, the next best option is to enlarge the print and photocopy the page. The student can then write on the photocopy and avoid the labor of copying. When neither of these options are available, be sure to provide the student with graph paper to line up his columns and spaces and to help him organize his work.

Simplify Word Problems
When presenting word problems, leave out any irrelevant information. The student with NLD will get so bogged down trying to make sense of this extraneous information that he may be unable to proceed with the problem. Have this child verbalize the process to you before any writing is attempted. He may not be able to show all of his work. This is okay, as long as he is reaching the correct solution. If not, again, ask him to verbalize to you how he arrived at his answer.

Use of Timed Tests
If you use timed tests (which actually have no value in assessing learning; neurological research contends that how quickly you can retrieve something is not related to how well you know it), be sure to reduce the number of problems and increase the amount of time allotted to the student with NLD. Provide ample work space on the paper for the student who needs to write BIG numbers. Timed tests cause frustration and anxiety for the student with NLD because of his visual-spatial-organizational difficulties and because of his slow rate of processing. How well a person knows something is not determined by how quickly he is able to do it. Ideally, timed tests should be eliminated entirely.

Electronic Alternatives
Since it is preferable that all students be permitted to work at their own pace, sequential computer programs can be used in place of timed tests. In most educational software developed for the classroom, the teacher has the option of programming in a preset number of problems for each student or the students can be allowed to advance on their own, once the computer determines they have mastered a concept. The student with NLD should be provided with earphones so that he is receiving the verbal input along with the visual display when working on a computer. For a student with graphomotor problems, it is much easier to tap a number on the keyboard than to go through the laborious process of writing it out.

Separate Writing Tasks from Math Learning

Be sure that you separate the written aspect of math instruction from the actual learning process. The student with NLD will progress faster if he is not required to do repetitive writing of material already learned (for example, if his understanding is clear from two or three problems, don't insist he complete ten — it then becomes nothing more than a frustrating writing exercise for him). He needs to concentrate so hard on forming the numbers, lining up the columns, and spacing the problems on his page that the assignment evolves into a writing chore and any learning of math concepts is actually undermined.

Geometry Considerations

The most difficult area of math instruction for the student with NLD is undoubtably geometry. This is because of the obvious visual-spatial attributes of this subject. Simultaneous processing, or processing all parts of a stimulus at once, is a function of the right hemisphere. Interpreting a map or a geometric figure involves simultaneous processing. It is often baffling for teachers to witness a student who had no difficulty with algebra (which requires successive processing, a left-hemisphere function) struggling with geometry. The child with NLD will find deciphering and drawing geometric figures extremely vexing. Multi-dimensional geometry is extremely difficult because of the child's muddled plane integration. It has been suggested that in planning a schedule for high school, the student with NLD be allowed to skip geometry and proceed directly on to Algebra II. This strategy has been successfully adapted in various high schools in Canada.

Organizational and Study Skills

Special Considerations

The student with NLD is usually highly capable of completing assignments that have been modified and adapted to his needs. But, all too often, he doesn't know how to get started, or he loses or misplaces his work, or he gets too bogged down with details (can't see the forest, only the trees — he doesn't comprehend the total assignment, only the particulars). This inability to get started on an assignment can be very frustrating for the student and for his teacher. A student with NLD has tremendous difficulty with temporal concepts (organizing time) and spatial perceptions (coordinating physical space). His classroom must be set up to accommodate these areas of need.

Reduce Visual Stimuli

To start with, check to make sure the classroom environment is not too visually stimulating. The student with NLD will have difficulty implementing structure in a sensorially overstimulating environment. An "open" classroom will probably prove to be too confusing. Constantly changing workgroups can be tormenting to a child with NLD. This child is unable to organize the internal structure these situations call for because he is on sensory overload. These conditions can cause undue stress and anxiety for the student. Organize his classroom so that the child has only one place where he works and only one place to turn in daily assignments. Keep all supplies for student use in one central area. In many instances, the student with NLD will perform better in a traditional, "everyone stays in their seats"-type classroom setting, provided there is plenty of time for one-on-one instruction and provided that appropriate CAMS for this child are in place.

Stick to the Schedule

Write the daily schedule on the board each day and try to always follow it. The student with NLD will need extra time to find and organize his materials at the start and finish of each new activity. Don't begin presenting new material while he is still coping with the previous lesson. He will miss your present instruction because he is still looking for the things he needs.

Any changes in scheduling or physical layout will lead to increased confusion, diminished problem-solving capacities, and ultimately leave the child with NLD feeling emotionally overwhelmed. He can't easily adjust to a shift in mental set. Allow more time for transitions and prepare the child for changes in routine. This child will be better equipped to deal with inconstant situations if he has been given adequate advance preparation.

Compensatory Strategies

Use the following strategies to help the child with NLD make it through the school day:

- Provide him with a simple map of the school. In the early grades, a buddy can help him get around and remember to turn in assignments.
- Help this student organize his desk or locker.
- Teach him how to prioritize assignments.
- Give him an extra set of textbooks to keep at home for previewing upcoming assignments.
- Teach the student to use self-talk to keep organized. He should be encouraged to verbalize the steps out loud until he is able to do it internally.

86 *The Source for Nonverbal Learning Disorders*

- Don't give multi-step directions because he can't visualize and will only become confused.

Emotional Concerns at School

The emotional abuse now often suffered by the child with NLD in some public and private schools is unconscionable in a society which strives to be compassionate of others. This child does not have the insight to realize that the teachers and other school officials who berate and reproach him are acting out of total ignorance. Instead, the child with NLD begins to believe that he is "bad" and that the constant castigation he receives from the adults around him must be deserved. Remember, he will not critically evaluate incoming information.

Eventually, this child may consider himself a complete failure — someone who can't do anything right. The fact that a child with NLD will so often ask, "What can I do to behave the way my teacher wants me to?" or "How can I make my teacher like me?" is indicative of his desire to conform and comply. This child, owing to his extreme vulnerability, can easily become the scapegoat of an unenlightened, frustrated teacher. A child with more fluid intelligence, what we know as "street smarts," would instinctively know how to "get on the good side" of his teachers. The fact that the child with NLD has to ask how to please his teacher, is an obvious tip-off that he lacks these competencies.

Likewise, peers can form the habit of teasing, bullying, and manipulating the child with NLD. This is where the attitude of the teacher and the rest of the school staff become crucial. The ability of the school staff to adapt their usual approach and accept their responsibilities toward the child with NLD, can make or break any intervention program designed to help the child. Prejudgments or a negative attitude by any member of the school staff toward a child with NLD will, unfortunately, give the other students license to tease and pick on this child, too. This type of tacit permission by authority figures sets up an abusive cycle that is impossible for the child to endure, day in and day out.

The Futility of Behavior Modification

Behavioral modification plans and behavior management techniques are an exercise in futility when imposed upon the child with NLD. He can't access the processes of his right-hemisphere and therefore has trouble figuring out what is expected of him, especially in new or novel circumstances (he generally knows black and white, it's the gray areas that give him difficulty). Just as you would not expect a blind child to be able to see, even if you were to work up an elaborate plan of rewards and punishments toward this end, it is ludicrous to believe that the child with NLD will be able to conform to your expectations, merely because a behavior management plan has been developed and implemented.

There is no harm in praising and rewarding desired behavior, but it is inappropriate and harmful to punish undesirable behavior which results from a neurological impairment (such as assigning detention for tardies to a child with severe visual-spatial-organizational difficulties). Please make sure the child with NLD isn't placed in a classroom which relies upon any type of visual classroom management system (such as names on the board, color-coded cards, etc.), which announce his difficulties to the world, but which offer no direct alternatives to him.

Traditional Behavior Modification Techniques	→	NLD Student's Anxiety Increases, Behavior is Unchanged
Calm, Helpful Verbal Strategies Employed	→	NLD Student's Anxiety Decreases, Behavior Improves

Furthermore, the student with NLD should not be asked to engage in a contract with his teachers and/or his parents that specifies rewards and penalties based upon his performance. This type of system will only serve to increase his already dangerous level of anxiety and undoubtedly prove to be self-defeating. When the correct strategies are employed to accommodate his right hemisphere deficiencies, the child with NLD becomes less anxious and his behavior generally improves without any other specific behavioral interventions. Punishment induces fear. Fear induces anxiety. Anxiety hinders performance. Do not force this child to fail.

Planning Considerations for the Child with NLD

The classroom teacher needs to schedule time each day to make changes in daily lesson plans (assignment modification, alternate testing procedures, etc.) for the student with NLD. As this teacher becomes more and more proficient, these planning sessions will take less time, but the daily frequency will still be required. During this planning time, the teacher should ask the following questions:

- "What are my goals and objectives for all my students in this area?"
- "How can this particular student successfully demonstrate these desired competencies?"
- "How can I modify my lesson plans to take into account this student's neurological syndrome?"

There are four basic techniques the teacher should consider when planning for the student with NLD in the classroom:

1. **Support** — this support should be designed to enable the student to benefit more fully from the classroom instruction and to successfully fulfill the requirements of the course, without necessarily completing every assignment.

   The teacher should prepare materials for previewing and determine appropriate supplemental aids (provision of a note-taker in class, a laptop computer at the student's desk, a cooperative group project, etc.) which can be used to provide the requisite support to the student with NLD.

2. **Adaptations** — the number of end products required of the student with NLD may need to be reduced, favoring quality over quantity. This student will probably require extra time to complete those assignments that are determined to be vital. And, even such indispensable assignments may need to be shortened or modified to contain fewer written responses. This is not a differential standard, but rather a different approach to meeting the same standards as the other students in the class.

   Assessment instruments must be reviewed to ensure that the method utilized will reflect what the student has learned and not penalize him for his neurological deficits. Also, grading criteria will probably need to be modified (especially in middle school and high school) for the student with NLD, keeping in mind that he may have followed a different path, but has reached the same final goal originally set by the teacher.

3. **Parallel Activities** — sometimes even previewing, supplemental aids, and reduced assignments aren't enough to modify the curriculum for a student with NLD. When it has been determined that an activity planned for the majority of students in a class may cause undue frustration for the student with NLD, a similar parallel activity should be created for him (and for other students who could also benefit). The alternate activity should fulfill the same functional curricular value as the original activity, but that alleviates the stress brought on by the limitations of his neurological syndrome. The parallel activity should be similar to the class activity and reinforce the same content of study. Here's an example of a parallel activity:

   A kindergarten teacher wishes to reinforce her students' knowledge of the alphabet with a cut and paste activity called "alpha-worm." The students are directed to cut out the letters of the alphabet which are randomly contained within squiggly lines on one paper and then to paste them in the correct sequence on another piece of paper to form an "alpha-worm."

The NLD student's fine-motor difficulties, coupled with his visual-spatial problems, make this activity especially grueling for him. So instead, the teacher creates a parallel activity which allows the student to demonstrate his knowledge of the correct sequence of the alphabet without becoming too bogged down by the cutting, visual-spatial arranging, and pasting of the class activity.

The NLD student is asked to recite the alphabet in sequence into a tape recorder. Then he is presented with four letters at a time on large cards (with no other visual distractions) and asked to point to a specific letter, to verify that he can identify the letter names. The student came through with flying colors and received full credit for the assignment.

4. **Modified Expectations** — the finished product for the student with NLD may not meet the same specific task expectations set forth for the majority of students, but may still meet the curricular goals and objectives for the course. The teacher, again, must focus on the desired curricular goals and determine which parts of the activity may be too demanding for this particular student. The following is an example of modified expectations:

The teacher's goal for a lesson is that the students will learn the names of the South American countries and their capitals. She prepares an overhead transparency with outlines of the countries and runs off a similar worksheet for the students. Her plan is to discuss each country and then write its name on the transparency for the students to copy. Then they will locate the capital and write its name on the corresponding nation. In this way, each student will have a completed map that he has contributed to, to take home and study.

For the student with NLD, who she knows will have difficulty copying from the overhead projector, the teacher provides a worksheet with the names of the countries and their capitals already written in. She walks by this student's desk, after writing on her transparency and physically points to the word on his worksheet. He is then asked to highlight the word with a highlighting marker. He also has a completed map to take home and study, without having to suffer through the painful process of copying from an overhead projector.

 The Source for Nonverbal Learning Disorders

Summary

As we have seen, classroom teachers play a crucial role in the integrated and carefully orchestrated program of intervention necessary for all students exhibiting the NLD syndrome. It is absolutely essential that everyone involved with this child be aware of the significance of NLD. The successful educational program of a student with NLD mandates a highly competent teacher (See the **Comparison of a Teacher and a Curriculum Imparter** on page 92.). This teacher must:

- Teach and not merely impart the curriculum.

- Individualize lesson plans and classroom procedures to accommodate the learning styles of individual students.

- Assess learning to determine grades (not count assignments).

- Be proactive (not reactive).

- See challenging behavior as a student's way of expressing a need — try to determine the need and fill it.

- Know that unique students don't purposefully set about to call attention to themselves (the phrase "attention getting behavior" is almost always a misnomer).

Students with NLD don't need their teachers to call attention to their difficulties in front of their peers. This singling out is the last thing such a child wants! All teachers must recognize and respect the child with NLD's desire to simply be like everyone else — even though there are times when he can't because of his neurological impairment. He deserves to be treated fairly (meaning his needs are met — without embarrassment to him). Any accommodations made for this child (such as extra time, modified assignments, alternate assessments, etc.) should be implemented discreetly within the classroom, and appear to be carried out for the benefit of the entire group, rather than just for a particular student.

The guidelines discussed in this chapter will not only profit the NLD student in a classroom, but will maximize the learning of all the students in that class. It is the NLD student's right to belong in the classroom. It is the job of the school's educational staff to provide the most appropriate program within the least restrictive environment.

Comparison of a Teacher and a Curriculum Imparter

A Teacher	A Curriculum Imparter
teaches	imparts curriculum
individualizes to accommodate learning styles of students	uses same delivery for all students
assesses learning to determine grades	counts assignments to determine grades
is proactive	is reactive
sees challenging behavior as a student's way of expressing a need — tries to determine the need and fill it.	uses the phrase "he/she chose to . . ." as an excuse for their own failure to familiarize themselves with a student's unique learning needs
knows that unique students don't wish to call attention to themselves	labels undesired behavior as "attention-getting"

Students need teachers — *not* curriculum imparters

            The Source for Nonverbal Learning Disorders

Summary of Tips and Strategies for Meeting the Child with NLD's Needs in the Classroom

General Classroom Tips

1. Minimize the number of adults working with this student. Communicate and collaborate daily.

2. Analyze student strengths and interests. This student learns through discussion. Don't isolate.

3. Monitor organizational skills daily. An assignment notebook helps organize and individualize.

4. Define processes in a linear, sequential format that can be memorized. (Don't expect "discovery" learning.)

5. Monitor and adjust assignments on a daily basis. Use alternate testing procedures as needed. Timed assignments only produce stress. Allow closure before moving to the next activity.

6. Previewing and supplemental aids (such as study guides, outlines, and audiocassettes of the material to be covered in class) allow this student to receive the maximum benefit from classroom instruction.

7. A positive attitude, enthusiasm for teaching, a sense of humor, and the willingness to make changes and adjustments in program are key components of a successful staff!

Reading Curriculum

1. This student should excel in reading programs which apply a guided, sequential, phonetic/linguistic approach to reading. Auditory cues will help this child learn new words.

2. A sequential approach is important. Make sure the student is allowed to move forward quickly once the required material is learned.

3. In the upper grades, provide outlines and notes of any material to be read. Allow this student to highlight these notes. Have the special education department purchase consumable texts for this student to mark in.

4. Comprehension difficulties will arise from hidden meanings. Teach and stress reading comprehension. Step-by-step guidance will be needed to help this student formulate answers to questions which are open-ended.

5. Allow extra time for reading assignments because of slow processing and visual-spatial difficulties. Don't require long stretches of continuous reading. Visual fatigue can result. Strive to minimize the number and length of reading assignments.

94 *The Source for Nonverbal Learning Disorder*

Written Language Curriculum

1. Written language calls on both right and left hemisphere functions. NLD is known to cause problems putting thoughts in writing.

2. An incapacity to cross information between the left and right hemispheres of the brain contributes to difficulty putting creative thoughts into writing.

3. The student has inadequate resources to even begin a typcial, grade-appropriate writing assignment. It may take him 10 minutes just to put his pencil to his paper.

4. Break down all written assignments and reports into the smallest possible component parts. Gradually work toward decreasing the mount of structure you provide.

5. Always look at the quality of a completed written assignment, rather than the quantity produced.

6. If the goal of the assignment isn't written language, allow the student to demonstrate his knowledge in an alternate format.

7. Provide the student with a word processor or computer to use on all lengthy written assignments.

Mathematics Curriculum

1. The visual-spatial nature of math activities often confuses the student with NLD. Problems arise in the areas of spatial organization, visual relationships, graphomotor deficiencies, and failure to generalize.

2. A step-by-step, structured, sequential approach will work best. Point out the similarities to this student that other students discover on their own. Don't ask this student to study an example in the text before you have given him a detailed verbal description of the process being illustrated.

3. Math instruction should *not* rely solely on drawings, diagrams, charts, and other visual displays. When demonstrating a new concept, explain each step in its sequential order verbally to the student.

4. Visual/tactile manipulatives add to this child's visual-spatial confusion, while at the same time, accentuating his poor planning abilities and fine-motor difficulties.

5. Math texts that rely upon lots of color and pictures can overwhelm the student. A simple layout with black-and-white text will be less visually confusing.

6. Purchase a consumable math text. Provide the student with graph paper to line up his columns and spaces and to help him organize his work.

7. When presenting word problems, leave out any irrelevant information.

8. Timed tests cause frustration and anxiety because of visual-spatial-organizational difficulties *and* because of slow processing. Ideally, timed tests should be eliminated.

9. Sequential computer programs can be used in place of times tests. The student should be provided with earphones.

10. Separate the written aspect of math instruction from the actual learning process.

11. The most difficult area of math is undoubtably geometry. Multi-dimensional geometry is a real killer because of muddled plane integration. If possible, have the student skip geometry and continue with advanced algebra instruction instead.

96 *The Source for Nonverbal Learning Disorders*

Spelling Curriculum

1. Spelling errors are usually phonetically accurate. Misspelled words are easily recognizable.

2. Don't ask this child to copy his spelling words from the chalkboard or to write them 10 times each. Repetitious writing won't reinforce his knowledge of a word's spelling.

3. This student may need parallel activities to practice spelling. Words presented visually should be supplemented with auditory prompting. Don't rely on visually confusing spelling reinforcement activities such as Bingo and word hunts.

4. Rhymes and songs can be taught to help this student remember the correct sequence of letters. Instead of paper and pencil tasks, let him practice his spelling words orally, or on tape.

5. Once the child knows how to spell a word, excessive repetition isn't necessary. Allow him to move on.

6. Although spelling instruction may prove redundant, let this child take spelling tests with his peers. Give him this chance to shine.

Organizational and Study Skills

1. The student with NLD is usually highly capable of completing assignments that have been modified and adapted to his needs. But all too often, he doesn't know how to get started, he loses or misplaces his work, or he gets too bogged down with details. His classroom must be set up to accommodate these areas of need.

2. Check to make sure the classroom environment isn't too visually stimulating. An "open" classroom will probably prove to be too confusing.

3. Write the daily schedule on the board each day and try to always follow it. Allow extra time for transitions.

4. Provide the student with a simple map of the school. Teach the student to use self-talk to keep organized. Don't give him multi-step directions because he can't visualize and will only become confused.

98   *The Source for Nonverbal Learning Disorders*

Chapter 7
An Appropriate Educational Placement
For the Child With NLD

Keeping in mind that all learning situations will require accommodations in curriculum and programming for the child with NLD, following are some suggested criteria to be aware of when considering an appropriate placement for this child . . .

Lisa's preschool teachers described her as "Trouble with a capital T!" With the cherubic face of a little blonde angel and the stubborn temper of a discontented mule, Lisa threw fits whenever the routine was changed at her school. She constantly talked back to the childcare workers, and she didn't get along well with the other children. As a result, Lisa spent a good part of her day at school in time out and complained loudly about how much she hated her school. The adults in charge grew increasingly irritated at her because Lisa always looked so confused when they reprimanded her over and over for doing the same things. And instead of apologizing for her misbehavior, Lisa would insist obstinately that she hadn't done anything wrong.

"I can see you've got your hands full with this one," one teacher confided to Lisa's single-parent mother.

With a conciliating sigh, Lisa's mom agreed. "I don't know what to do with her, either. She's so bossy with everyone and she doesn't know how to make friends. But would you believe that the two of us get along fine when we're at home alone together — providing I have the time to answer all her questions."

Besides inconsistencies in Lisa's behavior at preschool and at home, other contradictions were also becoming obvious to Lisa's mother. Although Lisa had rolled-over, sat-up, and walked at all the "right" developmental times, her balance always seemed to be faulty. She would bump into walls and other objects, usually from her left side. As a result, Lisa was constantly covered with bruises. And, Lisa couldn't quite manage to stay up on her bicycle, despite her intense dedication toward mastering her balance.

"Slow down and pay attention to what you're doing," Lisa's mom would caution her. But her mother's pleas didn't help. A consultation with Lisa's pediatrician at age four led to the diagnosis of AD/HD. Lisa was prescribed Ritalin and seemed to settle down somewhat. So it was disheartening to find that what her teachers labeled "behavior problems" continued in kindergarten.

Lisa's mother tearfully admitted to me, "There were so many days when I just wanted to keep her home from school with me, to protect her from all the cruel things that the other students would say and do to her. And as far as I'm concerned, her kindergarten teacher was no better than the five-year-old students. She was always making an example of Lisa — holding her up for display. Other students were told, 'You don't want to be like Lisa, do you?' when the teacher wanted to warn them not to mis-behave."

Rescuing Lisa

At the end of that school year, Lisa and her mother moved and were relocated within another school district. That summer, Lisa's mother became involved with the volunteer organization CH.A.D.D. (Children and Adults with Attention Deficit Disorder) and learned about some of the rights her daughter was entitled to under the special education laws. When Lisa's mother enrolled Lisa in first grade at her new school, she requested special education intervention because of her daughter's AD/HD diagnosis. Assessment forms were signed and the school's team evaluated Lisa.

The school psychologist reported to Lisa's mom, "Your daughter clearly has a nonverbal learning disorder." He pointed out a significant discrep-ancy between Lisa's verbal and performance IQ's and went on to explain how Lisa's early history and current symptoms fit the profile of a child with NLD. Lisa's mother couldn't believe that there was actually an identifiable syndrome that explained all the inconsistencies she'd been observing in Lisa. The school special education assessment team deter-mined that Lisa's needs could still be met with inclusive schooling. They got together with her mother and developed an IEP for Lisa which speci-fied a number of accommodations which they all agreed were necessary for Lisa's future success. The team was careful to thoroughly address all the areas affected by Lisa's NLD. The resulting IEP was quite compre-hensive (24 pages).

Even prior to the development of her IEP, Lisa was already having a more successful year in first grade than she had had with any of her previous school experiences. At first, her mother attributed the changes in Lisa's adjustment to her Ritalin. But once the IEP was put into place, it became obvious that the educational interventions were just as impor-tant to Lisa's success as the pharmaceutical intervention. Lisa was really beginning to soar. The specific modifications being implemented daily in her classroom allowed Lisa to feel a part of her first grade group. With a teacher who knew that humiliation and punishment weren't the answers, Lisa could show the world what a capable and endearing stu-dent she really could be.

Lisa's first grade teacher, Miss Rose, was exceptional in many respects. All the modifications and accommodations enacted for Lisa's benefit were implemented in such a manner that none of the other students even knew Lisa was being accommodated. Individual support was arranged with discretion and creativity. Changes in school activities which were put into place expressly for Lisa, such as "lunch club," individual assignment books, a "permanent" substitute teacher, and pencil grips were all seen to be organized for the group, rather than just for Lisa.

This teacher made a concerted effort to always prepare Lisa for changes in routine, but she never singled Lisa out or embarrassed her in front of the other students. Miss Rose provided Lisa's mother with information about topics of study in advance, so that she could preview the information with Lisa ahead of time. In addition, Miss Rose set up situations where Lisa could exercise her strong verbal skills to socialize with her peers. Lisa was assigned to be a "reader," a student who helped the non-readers in the class by reading instructions and notes to them. And, she was given the job of sorting the reading cards and placing them in a pocket chart before each reading period. This made Lisa feel very important!

"Lunch club" was a solution the IEP team devised to help alleviate Lisa's cafeteria and playground problems at lunchtime. A first grade lunch club was formed to provide a respite for Lisa. Three or four students were allowed to eat their lunches in the classroom with their teacher and play together quietly afterwards. Some days Lisa tutored the other students to help them with their reading and other days they played a board game or worked on the class computer.

Individual assignment books allowed Miss Rose to modify Lisa's written assignments without the other students asking why Lisa didn't have to do the same amount of written work as they did. And, pencil grips were available for any student who wanted one. The students with dysgraphic tendencies (and Lisa was not the only one) were given extra encouragement to use them. None of the students, however, was told that the special education department had actually purchased the pencil grips for Lisa's benefit.

Miss Rose requested that the same substitute be assigned to her class whenever she needed to be out and made a point of introducing the "permanent" substitute teacher to the entire class early in the year (thanks to a very cooperative school district, this was possible and benefited all of the students in the class). If Miss Rose needed to be out on a particular day and hadn't had time beforehand to prepare her students, this wonderful teacher made sure that she called Lisa's home right after she called for the substitute. In that way, Lisa didn't arrive at school unprepared for a change in routine.

Lisa's IEP called for a monthly conference time to give Lisa's mom a forum to express her concerns to the staff and to give the staff an opportunity to discuss Lisa's progress with her mother. It was agreed ahead of time that these conferences would not be "tattle" sessions and they never were. Although some specific problems did arise in the course of the school year, especially with changes in routine, Lisa's mother was given predominantly positive feedback, which she felt helped improve her interactions at home with her daughter. And, she confessed, it was nice to finally be hearing "good things" about the little girl she loved so much, instead of always hearing only "bad things."

The staff at Lisa's new school was a real gift. If it weren't for a very informed school psychologist familiar with NLD and appropriate interventions for a child with NLD, and a very supportive teacher willing to modify her whole program in order to assist Lisa, the prognosis for Lisa, at that point in her life, would probably have been quite poor. Lisa could easily have been labeled a "bad child" and subjected to reproach, from teachers and peers alike, for years to come.

As it stands, Lisa is now a fully-included third grader at that same school. She has been off Ritalin for over a year. She spends her free time with two close girl friends her age, and she receives excellent report cards. Lisa now has lunch with the rest of the students in her class. In fact, by the end of her first grade year, Lisa asked if she could play out on the playground some days. Her teacher always sent her out with a buddy and made sure that Lisa knew she could return to the classroom if she encountered any problems.

The yard duty staff was alerted to carefully watch the other children, to be sure they didn't tease or pick on Lisa. By second grade, Lisa no longer needed the lunch club, but the option was left open to her, and on days when she felt a little anxious, she stayed in with her teacher. None of the other students ever knew the lunch club was formed to comply with Lisa's IEP. Her extensive IEP follows Lisa, with updates and revisions for progress, annually. Hopefully, her future schooling will build on these early successes. Lisa's early diagnosis and subsequent appropriate intervention is evidence that the earlier the intervention, the better the chances for a positive outcome.

Parents' Roles in Educational Placement

Parents need to take an active role in ensuring that their child with NLD receives an appropriate education in the least restrictive environment. It usually falls upon the parents to insist that all staff involved with their child understand and provide assistance for her unique needs and to guard against inappropriate behavioral interventions. It also is the parents' responsibility to take steps to help prepare their child with NLD for the adjustments of attending school.

Since the child with NLD is unable to project and to apply previously learned information to new situations, she likes to keep all the variables in her life predictable. You can help prepare your child for the changes she'll encounter in a school environment by introducing new events gradually, at a pace she can cope with, not all at once. Prior to the first day of school, you may want to:

- make an advance visit to the school at a time when you can stay with your child to help her become familiar with the routine

- inspect the environment and verbally point out the bathrooms, quiet and play areas, playground boundaries, etc.

- discuss school rules with your child which are different from those you have at home

- meet with her new teacher and/or some of her classmates to help familiarize your child with the new people she will encounter

Educational Setting Considerations

If all school assessment teams were as knowledgeable, and all teachers were as compassionate and accommodating as those at Lisa's school, admittedly parents could let up a little and assume that the educational professionals in their child's life would do their jobs properly. Unfortunately, though, Lisa's preschool and kindergarten experiences are more typical of the rampant abuse encountered by children with NLD upon entering school. Keeping in mind that all classrooms will need to make supportive accommodations in curriculum and programming for the child with NLD, following are some suggested criteria to be aware of when considering an appropriate placement for this child.

Preschool

A small class size will be beneficial for the child with NLD, but *too few* children can further impede this child's social development. Somewhere between 6-12 children is usually appropriate. From as early an age as possible, the child with NLD needs to be around other children who interact in a suitable manner and who use appropriate social skills. It is essential that her peers be verbal, as she will not learn from the nonverbal interactions of others (children with NLD placed in communicably handicapped programs are generally left confused and frustrated by the flurry of nonverbal behaviors evidenced by children who have difficulty communicating verbally). For these reasons, most special education programs will prove to be too restrictive and will not meet the needs of the child with NLD.

Montessori programs are also generally not recommended for the child with NLD because there is limited opportunity for social interaction within that structure. At a Montessori preschool, the children are usually encouraged, and in some cases required, to work individually, which is not advantageous for the child with NLD during this period of her development. Although she will probably be captivated by the attention to routine a Montessori preschool adheres to, the emphasis on reading skills, and the prevalence of rotely memorized material (geography: names of countries, states, land formations; geometry: names of obscure shapes; details of biology: plant parts, leaf types, etc.), the child with NLD will probably also experience a high degree of frustration by the complexity of the many manipulatives requiring fine-motor coordination, the restrictive posture of working on a small swatch of carpet (which requires a body awareness not possible for the child with NLD) and the visual-spatial confusion generated by lots of multi-dimensional apparatus.

An Appropriate Preschool Setting

An appropriate preschool program for a child with NLD will stress these components:

- sensory-motor experiences
- structured play experiences
- lots of opportunities for organized social interaction

Although this child is probably reading beyond the level of her peers and is very talkative, an academically-based program will only reinforce her areas of strength and will not properly address the areas of deficit which require intervention. Programs which emphasize a lot of large group instruction, with little one-on-one teaching will also not prove conducive to this child's learning style. Look for these contingencies in an appropriate preschool setting:

- The staff should be limited and consistent.
- The child with NLD should remain with the same group of children and teacher(s) for at least an entire year (longer is preferable).
- Supplemental occupational therapy is recommended, as early as possible, for a child with low muscle tone and coordination difficulties.

The main considerations when evaluating the desirability of any preschool program should be:

- the willingness of the staff to accommodate your child's needs

104 *The Source for Nonverbal Learning Disorders*

- the acceptance and nurturing attitude of both the staff and the other children toward your child

- the opportunities for positive social interactions available to your child

If these three elements exist, everything else can be worked around. (Note: Presently a large majority of the children with NLD have not yet been identified when they enter a preschool setting. Although they already may be experiencing difficulties, their problems are usually thought to be behavioral in nature. The preceding recommendations are based on the hopes that this situation will change in the near future, as parents become more aware of NLD and professionals become more competent at recognizing these children.)

Primary Years

Again, the child with NLD should spend as much time as possible in regular education programs. Most special day class programs are set up to accommodate the needs of children exhibiting much more uniform developmental disabilities. The child with NLD will probably be automatically precluded from such placements, in any case, owing to her strong reading and verbal skills. A kindergarten class of 12-18 children, and elementary classes of no more than 25 students, will provide a conducive atmosphere for learning and socialization for this child.

Although the child with NLD needs sufficient opportunities to associate with a peer group, this child can be overwhelmed by too much input (especially if it is of a nonverbal nature). Unstructured segments of the day will cause the greatest difficulties for a child with NLD. Teasing and bullying of this child need to be taken seriously by the entire school staff. The best strategy to avoid these problems is careful planning beforehand. Protection of the child should come ahead of exposure. The lunch club is a perfect example of a strategy to avoid the playground difficulties a child with NLD may encounter. Resource help, such as an inclusion assistant in the regular classroom, can be beneficial to the success of placements made in a regular program.

Using an Inclusion Assistant

An inclusion assistant should be trained to exercise discretion in her interactions with the child. It is not in the child's best interest, and probably not helpful at all, to merely have an adult sitting next to her pointing out her mistakes all day. Talk about stress! The inclusion assistant can be used in small groups which include the child with NLD. Small group work is always preferable for this child, in any case. Alternatively, the inclusion assistant can support the child with NLD by working with a different group of children within the classroom, freeing up the teacher to give more individual support to this child. The classroom teacher then has the flexibility she needs to monitor and adjust assignments for the student with NLD. Or, the inclusion assistant could have no direct contact with that particular student at all, but rather could assist the teacher in preparation of:

- *previewing* for the student (presenting the student with materials to familiarize him with the subject matter before class instruction or a test)

- *supportive teaching* (making accommodations and modifications which allow a special education student to experience success in a regular classroom)

- *alternate assessments* (an evaluation using methods other than those applied to the majority of students in a class to assess a particular student's knowledge)

Classroom Environment

The classroom routine for this child should be structured and predictable, but not rigid. The child with NLD will perform better in an environment where she can usually anticipate what is going to happen next. She must have a teacher who can accommodate her unique learning style in an amenable, compassionate, and discreet manner (Miss Rose was perfect for Lisa!). The teacher will need to use this child's verbal strengths and rote memory to support her weaker areas. And, the teacher should also be involved in the process of directly teaching appropriate social skills.

Providing a child with NLD with a small "job" in the classroom, preferably one that capitalizes on her strong verbal skills, to do on her own (or with one other student) on a regular basis, will help build up her confidence and self-esteem. Choose jobs which are rewarding to the student, not too demanding, and don't involve more than one other student (peer tutoring and sorting the reading flash cards were excellent choices for Lisa in first grade). When the other students realize that their teacher relies upon this child, they become more tolerant of her other "annoying" behaviors.

If a Sensory Integrative Therapy program is available at the child's elementary school, she should be involved in this program. Occupational therapy will continue to be of importance, especially in dealing with the perceptual,

DEFINITION

Sensory Integrative Therapy
developed by Dr. Jean Ayres, an occupational therapy treatment program consisting of exercises which encourage the individual to use as many nerve-cell connections as possible

 The Source for Nonverbal Learning Disorders

coordination, and sensory-motor deficits which exacerbate dysgraphia. Adaptive P.E. is another consideration at school. Speech and language pathologists should work directly with the student with NLD on language pragmatics and, also, be available for consultation with the child's classroom teacher. The student with NLD should not be expected to get herself to her support services on her own, but rather she should be collected or brought to the correct room.

The school's Resource Specialist or school psychologist should arrange regular consultation times with the child's classroom teacher to ensure that the intervention program in place continues to meet both the educational and the social needs of this child. Regular parent contact, which is positive and informative, will facilitate school/home relations. The child should not be additionally burdened by being put in the position of a "go-between," delivering messages between home and school. Vital information should be conveyed by phone or mail. This child needs less stress, not more.

Diligence must be employed by the school staff in order to safeguard the child with NLD from becoming a scapegoat of her peer group. Remember, she doesn't have access to the competencies which would allow her to offset scapegoating from occurring, on her own. Parent involvement in troubleshooting these potentially damaging situations is also often necessary.

Placement in a special day class for Severely Emotionally Disturbed students (SED class) is usually inappropriate and detrimental for the child with nonverbal learning disabilities. Since her behavioral manifestations result from a neurological disorder, once the appropriate interventions are implemented within a regular classroom setting, the behavioral issues generally recede and the child's ability to function within the mainstream improves. Although some children with NLD will require placement in special classes for a time, the majority can manage in the mainstream if appropriate CAMS and individual support are provided. A caring and nonpunitive staff is imperative, as is a staff knowledgeable of NLD.

Middle School

Middle school is usually the most difficult transition for the child with NLD. A study hall should be built into this student's schedule to allow extra time for gathering thoughts and completing assignments. Modified school days (i.e. the student goes home at lunch time) may be necessary to ease the transition from one teacher to five or six teachers.

Nightly homework, for the most part, should be eliminated. If the student is learning and progressing in her classes, she needs the time outside of school to unwind and develop socialization skills. This child has undoubtably exhausted all of her powers of concentration just to get through a complicated day at school. What generally happens is that this student gets so bogged down with reading and written work after school, she is forced to sever all contacts with friends and all participation in extracurricular activities. This is extremely unhealthy and is also often the trigger for a major depressive episode.

Middle school is also the time when great caution needs to be exercised in enforcing disciplinary regulations. The child with NLD is functioning with a different set of competencies than most of her peers. It is, therefore, mandatory that this student not be punished or singled-out for behaviors which result from her areas of incompetency. Rarely will this child engage in grossly maladjusted behavior. The more likely scenario is a preponderance of misjudgments and misinterpretations of expectations. These incidents should be handled compassionately, educating the child, rather than penalizing her.

High School

Often an improvement is seen in both academics and social behavior in high school because the child has "bottomed-out" in middle school and is finally now receiving appropriate CAMS. Unfortunately, students with NLD who have not been identified and appropriately serviced by the time they reach high school may be forced to drop out.

Be careful that this child is not placed in an SED class or a continuation program which is set up largely for students with behavioral disorders. NLD is not an emotional or a behavioral disorder: it involves a neurological dysfunction. Inclusive schooling, with a well developed IEP, is still the most appropriate placement. A computer should be provided for this student both at school and at home, for written work. Every staff member involved with this child needs inservice training and ongoing guidance in order to provide an appropriate program for her.

108   *The Source for Nonverbal Learning Disorders*

Chapter 8
Compensations, Accommodations, Modifications, and Strategies

Ideally, the parents, teachers, and all other professionals involved with a child with NLD will all work together to develop a program which helps this child to reach her fullest potential . . .

Mallory's learning style was clearly different from that of most of the other children I worked with at the time I met her. Her behavior was also quite different. Mallory was a tall, well-developed fourth-grader, with an Irish mother and Italian father. Her olive skin, thick black lashes, and dark curly hair gave her the striking features of a fashion model. While the other girls her age were passing through an awkward, gangly, pre-puberty stage, Mallory appeared mature beyond her years. But looks can be deceptive. Notwithstanding her stunning appearance, Mallory was lacking in social skills and was constantly in trouble at school. Her difficulties completing written work, despite a high intelligence, eventually placed her in my Resource Specialist Program. What I saw was a student who really wanted to do better, but couldn't seem to keep up. Her immature and, at times, unexplainable behavior exasperated all who knew her.

Early in the school year, a conference was arranged by the school psychologist with Mallory's mother. I attended, as did the school principal and vice-principal (both of whom had seen Mallory on numerous occasions for disciplinary reasons). We learned from a teary-eyed mother that ten-year-old Mallory was her fourth daughter, and that her other three children were all in their twenties, married, and living on their own. There was a twelve-year age difference between Mallory and her next youngest sister. So, in essence, Mallory was an only child of two middle-aged parents who doted over her constantly. It was easy to draw the conclusion that she was over-indulged at home and that she didn't comply with the rules at school because she was allowed to get away with things at home.

In the course of our conference, Mallory's mother divulged that she felt Mallory demonstrated less savvy than her other daughters had shown at the same age. Mallory's mother admitted that she tended to be over-protective with Mallory, but she defended her actions, stating that she felt Mallory required an extra amount of parental guidance. She told us that Mallory just didn't pick up the social cues that she should and that other children often took advantage of her.

The mother described how she and her husband arranged their work schedules so that one of them was always home with Mallory. If she wanted to visit a friend's house, they arranged to take Mallory there and pick her up, because she often got lost going places on her own. Her mother knew that some of the other parents felt that she and her husband were "babying" Mallory, but something inside of her told Mallory's mother that Mallory needed this uncommon vigilance.

With the information that he had available, the school psychologist concluded that Mallory didn't show the maturity of her peers because her parents had not allowed her to function independently. A ten-year-old should be able to visit her friends without her parents' constant interference, the psychologist related. He and the school principal suggested to the mother that, starting immediately, Mallory should be allowed to visit with her friends after school, without checking in first with her parents. The psychologist also urged that her parents let Mallory learn to stick up for herself and that they should expect a few hard knocks along the way. "She'll only learn if you let go and force her to be independent," he counseled. Mallory's mother agreed that she had not been so protective with her other daughters, and that they were all now healthy, happy, independent adults.

The new plan went into effect the next day. But, instead of hanging out with friends her own age, as everyone had hoped, Mallory began hanging out at a taco shop near her home. She "made friends" with the manager, who offered to pay her for coming in after school and sweeping the floor and washing off the tables. Mallory was thrilled. Her parents were also delighted that Mallory not only seemed to be becoming more independent, but also that she was earning some spending money for herself. Everyone felt the plan proposed by the school psychologist was right on target . . . until, in the ensuing months, Mallory's mother noticed her daughter becoming very withdrawn at home.

Mallory stopped talking to her parents and shut herself in her room whenever she was home. When she stopped eating and lost nearly 20 pounds from her already slender frame, her parents were at a loss to know what to do. They contacted the school psychologist who recommended that they take Mallory to see her pediatrician about a possible eating disorder. Eventually, the whole ugly, frightening story came out. Mallory had been raped . . . not once, but several times by her "friend" at the taco shop. She had also been tied up and videotaped during the ordeal.

Mallory trusted the manager at the taco shop because the man was nice to her, and because he gave her a job. She even continued coming to see him after school, because he told her she had to. It could be argued that Mallory didn't have the social skills to read this person because she had been so over-protected by her parents. But, those who knew her, knew that Mallory had always had difficulty reading people and interacting appropriately in social situations. Mallory's mother's instincts were correct. Her daughter didn't have the social maturity to be as independent as the other children her age.

 The Source for Nonverbal Learning Disorders

Mallory's parents left the area with her shortly after her rape was discovered. I don't know if Mallory was ever officially diagnosed with NLD, but her unconditional trust and naivete in social situations mirrors the behavior of a child with NLD. Similar horrific incidents involving males with NLD have come to my attention, also. Mallory's experience is a very extreme example, but one which bears retelling, if only to caution caregivers to follow their instincts.

If the child you're entrusted with seems naive, overly trusting, or unable to determine the motives of others (and this will be evident early on), don't push this child to be independent. Carefully structure all social situations, and slowly loosen your ties; do not abruptly leave this child to sink or swim, regardless of any professional advice to the contrary that you may receive. The child with NLD processes incoming information very differently from the way most children do.

Ideally, the parents, teachers, and all other professionals involved with a child with NLD will all work together to develop a program which helps this child to reach her fullest potential by recognizing and compensating her areas of disability, while at the same time, allowing her to capitalize on her strong verbal strengths. Although each child with NLD presents a slightly different picture, there are enough similarities among these children that CAMS which are developed for one have proven effective for others, also.

Compensations

1. **Help this child by allowing her extra time to get places and by giving her verbal cues to navigate through space.** This child will have difficulties with internal and external organization and coordination. Tardiness is something she may struggle with (despite great pains to be punctual), and this should not be treated as misbehavior. Continually assess her understanding of spatial and directional concepts.

2. **Never underestimate the gravity of this disability.** Dr. Rourke states that "One of the most frequent criticisms of remedial intervention programs with this particular type of child is that the remedial authorities are unaware of the extent and significance of the child's deficits," and he emphasizes that "the principal impediment to engaging in this rather slow and painstaking approach to teaching the child with NLD is the caregiver's (faulty) impression that the child is much more adept and adaptable than is actually the case." Dr. Rourke also warns that, "Observers tend to overvalue the 'intelligence' of NLD adolescents . . . [and] this is the principal reason for an

unwillingness to adopt an approach to formal educational intervention that would increase the NLD youngster's probability of success."

The naivete of parents and educators regarding the significance of the NLD syndrome inevitably leads to inappropriate expectations being placed upon this child. Expectations for this child should always be applied with flexibility, taking into consideration the fact that she has different needs and abilities than her peer group. (Note: This individual's progress is almost always further impeded by anosognosia — the "virtual inability to reflect on the nature and seriousness of [her own] problems").

DEFINITION

anosognosia
the virtual inability to reflect on the nature and seriousness of one's own problems (a characteristic exhibited by many children with NLD which prevents them from recognizing differences between themselves and their peers)

---

3. **Don't force independence on this child, if you sense she is not yet ready for something (trust your instincts and be careful not to compare her with other children of the same age).** It is detrimental to isolate her, but don't make the mistake of thinking she can be left to her own resources when faced with new and/or complex situations. Give her verbal compensatory strategies to deal more effectively with novel situations. The world can be very confusing and downright scary for someone who is misreading at least 65% of all communication. This child will naturally be reluctant to try new things. Her social skill development has been delayed by misconceptions which may have caused serious issues of insecurity to evolve.

The myth of the "overprotective mother" needs to be dismissed (remember Mallory's mother — she knew her daughter's needs better than anyone); parents and professionals must both assume a protective and helpful role when working with the child with NLD. Dr. Rourke states that "Although sensitive caregivers are often accused of 'overprotection,' it is clear that they may be the only ones who have an appreciation for the child's vulnerability and lack of appropriate skill development."

Care and discretion need to be taken to shield the child from teasing, persecution, and other sources of anxiety. Independence should be introduced gradually, in controlled, non-threatening situations. The more completely those around her understand this child and her particular strengths and weaknesses, the better prepared they will be to promote attitudes of personal independence. *Never leave this child to her own devices in new activities or situations which lack sufficient structure.*

112 *The Source for Nonverbal Learning Disorders*

4. **Avoid power struggles, criticism, punishment, and threatening. All types of negative reinforcements need to be avoided.** This child doesn't understand rigid displays of authority and anger. Avoid shouting at her; it will only add to her confusion. Threats such as, "if you do _____, then _____ will happen to you," only destroy this child's sense of hope and make her feel she is a "bad" person, if she is unable to follow through. The goals and expectations assigned to this child must be attainable and worthwhile.

Remember that taking away privileges won't cure a child of a neurological dysfunction (but may very well establish her on the path to depression). Negative reinforcements are inappropriate intervention models on the part of the adults involved and will prove to be detrimental and damaging to this child's development and well-being. When a child's waking hours consist of one punishing experience after another, it is only natural that she stops caring, and eventually stops trying. The confusion and social awkwardness the child with NLD displays are *real* and unintentional; they should never be viewed as conduct to be penalized.

5. **All adults owe it to this child to always assume the best; to always take a positive rather than a negative approach.** As we have seen, life is very demanding and difficult for the child with NLD. Most of her unusual behavioral responses serve a purpose and usually represent the child's own attempt at compensation. No child chooses to solicit your disapproval.

It is wise to try to uncover the reason for the behavior and to help the child devise an appropriate (more acceptable) replacement behavior (usually through a detailed verbal explanation). Parents and professionals need to make the effort to have the child explain his dilemma and to try to uncover the purpose his behavior might be serving. After determining the rationale behind the child's actions, parents and educators should seek to *serve the child's need*, rather than punishing the resulting behavior. Remember, as with all children, at least 90% of your interactions with this child must be positive in nature!

Accommodations

1. **School assignments which require merely copying text need to be modified or omitted, owing to the visual-spatial nature of such an exercise.** Active verbalization and/or subvocalization are the best memory approaches for this child.

2. **Test answer sheet layouts and the arrangement of visual-spatial math assignments need to be simplified (no credit should be lost for a correct answer placed in the wrong column or space).** Whenever possible, use of graph paper is recommended to help keep columns properly aligned in written math assignments or (even better) consumable math texts should be provided for this student. Using pre-lined paper that helps this child better configure her work space is advised.

3. **Paper and pencil tasks need to be kept to a minimum because of finger dexterity and visual-spatial problems.** Occupational therapy is a consideration for the younger child. Verbally mediated practices to improve handwriting may result in improvements in control and fluency, but the process will remain laborious.

   Use of a computer word processor is highly recommended for all written school assignments, as the spatial and fine motor skills needed for typing are not as complicated as those involved in handwriting. This will also allow her to write in rough draft and more easily edit and self-correct.

4. **The global confusions which underlie nonverbal learning disorders also result in limiting the student's ability to produce the quantity of written work normally expected of her grade level peers.** This child requires continuous assistance in organizing information and communicating in writing.

   Creative writing assignments can be wrought with anxiety. To ease the process of writing, you should follow these tips:
   - Help the student with NLD develop her creative skills by drawing on real-life experiences.
   - Make adjustments in teacher expectations for volume of written products.
   - Provide additional time for all written assignments.

114 *The Source for Nonverbal Learning Disorde*

5. **Tasks requiring folding, cutting with scissors, or arranging material in a visual-spatial manner (maps, graphs, mobiles, etc.) will require considerable assistance, provided in an accommodating manner, or they *should be eliminated entirely*.** It is important that the child with NLD be placed in small cooperative groupings, or with a buddy, for help with art and science projects.

6. **Any timed assignments will need to be modified or eliminated.** Processing of all information is performed at a much slower rate when you are compensating for any type of cerebral dysfunction. Time constraints often prove to be highly counterproductive, as this student is easily overwhelmed by the unrealistic expectations of her teachers.

7. **Adults need to check often for understanding and present information in plain and clear verbal terms (i.e. "spell out" everything).** A "parts-to-whole" verbal teaching approach should be utilized. This child will need to ask a lot of questions, as this is her primary means of gathering information.

8. **All expectations need to be direct and explicit (don't require this child to "read between the lines" to glean your intentions).** Use short sentences for directives. Avoid abstract terms, sarcasm, figurative speech, idioms, slang, etc., unless you plan to explain your usage. *Verbal directions and explanations should accompany all instructions.*

   Write exact expectations for any situation where the child may seriously misperceive complex directions and/or proper social cues. The child with NLD usually has an extensive vocabulary at her disposal, but she will still have difficulty comprehending abstract concepts, idioms, and words with multiple meanings. Feedback given to the student should always be constructive and encouraging, or there will be no benefits derived.

9. **This student's schedule needs to be as predictable as possible.** In elementary school, set a specific routine for starting the day which involves a preview of what the child can expect throughout the day. Once the child feels comfortable within the set routine, gradually introduce variations. Let the child develop a sense of security before expecting her to develop more flexibility. This child should always be prepared in advance for changes in routine, such as assemblies, field trips, minimum days, vacation days, finals, etc. One announcement may not be enough. Continue to provide verbal and written reminders right up to the time of the change in routine.

10. **Assign one case manager at school who will oversee this child's progress and assure that all of the school staff are implementing the necessary accommodations and modifications.** Inservice training and orientation for all school staff that promotes tolerance and acceptance is a vital part of the overall plan for success, as everyone must be familiar with, and supportive of, the child's academic and social needs.

Modifications

1. **The child with NLD needs to be in a learning environment that provides daily, non-threatening contact with non-disabled peers (i.e. not a "special" or "alternative" program) in order to further her social development.**

2. **This child will benefit from cooperative learning situations (when grouped with good role models).** Placing the child with NLD within a small group of children who can model acceptable interpersonal interactions provides an excellent opportunity for her to acquire appropriate social skills. Active verbalization is an important element in how this child learns.

   The child with NLD usually has extensive verbal information to share with the others and can be exposed to the give-and-take of a miniature social environment in a non-threatening, controlled milieu. This type of approach to learning not only increases the child's opportunities for social interaction, but also can serve to increase the acceptance of this child by her peers.

   Obviously, the child with nonverbal learning disorders would not be expected to be the "scribe" in a cooperative grouping; her contribution should be in the verbal arena. Always grouping the child with NLD with other children who use appropriate social skills is a crucial component of the modifications parents and teachers must implement.

   The least effective learning model for this child is working in isolation (she must be allowed to verbalize and to receive verbal feedback from others in order to learn).

3. **Transitions will always be difficult for this child, so she will need time during the school day to collect her thoughts before switching gears.** Try the following to help ease transitions situations:
   - Provide extra time before and after breaks to disengage and readjust to the changes in pace.

- Eliminate frequent changing of rooms and have the child spend more time with one teacher
- Include a study hall in this student's schedule at middle and high school levels
- Assign a carefully selected non-NLD peer buddy to help guide the student with NLD through her day.

4. **Placement must be in an environment which has a well-established routine because this child will not decipher nonverbal cues.** Limit the number of adults who come into contact with the child each day. The fewer personalities she has to adapt to, the less anxious she will be. She can't adjust well to constant changes in routine (this child lacks the ability to "wing it" in times of doubt) and has learned to fear all new and/or unknown situations and experiences. She needs to know what will happen next and to be able to count on consistent responses from the staff who work with her.

5. **Special presentation procedures need to be adapted for those subjects requiring visual-spatial-organizational and/or nonverbal problem-solving skills.** Or, as Dr. Rourke suggests, "avoid such material altogether." Divide long-term projects into small, easily assimilated segments. Establish a specific time frame for each segment. This student needs to receive appropriate feedback for the completion of each segment. *All repetitive-rote homework must be eliminated.*

Strategies

1. *Do* tell this child *everything* **and encourage her to give you verbal feedback.** Expect rote learning to come before applied learning. The most effective instructional procedures are those that associate verbal labels with concrete situations and experiences. The phrase, "I shouldn't have to tell you . . ." does not apply; assume you do have to tell her. You need to tell her *what, when, where, why,* and *how* — and have her feed it back to you. She can't look and learn.

An effective four-step strategy (for both parents and teachers) working with a child with NLD follows:

1. You model a task for the child, providing a verbal description of exactly what you are doing while completing the task.

2. Verbally break the task down into its component parts and present each step sequentially, with its verbal label. Leave out irrelevant asides. Try to speak in concrete terms.

3. Guide the child through the task and assist her in acquiring the verbal self-talk to guide herself through it.

4. Let the child complete the task on her own, talking herself through it.

She will *not* visualize the task in her mind. Therefore, she needs to remember the verbal sequence you gave her. Be sure your feedback is clear and concise. Don't expect her to fill in the blanks . . . nothing is intrinsically understood.

2. **Verbally teach (don't expect the child to observe) cognitive strategies for the skills of conversational pragmatics and nonverbal body language.** Some language components of pragmatics iclude the following:

   - the give-and-take and comfortable beginnings and endings of a conversation

   - how and when to change the subject

   - formal versus informal conversational idiosyncrasies

   - tone and expression of voice

   Nonverbal body language includes:

   - facial expressions

   - correct social distance

   - knowing when the limit or cut-off point has been reached

   - tension and/or relaxation

   This child will *not* perceive that she is trying someone's patience until that person verbally explodes (and then the child is genuinely shocked and hurt)! Give her some additional verbal cues before the boiling point is reached because she can't "sense" tension or displeasure.

                                   The Source for Nonverbal Learning Disorders

3. **Help this child develop her own abstract language skills by always commenting on what was *meant* by a particular phrase or statement, as it's used.** Also, give her the benefit of the doubt when she fails to adequately explain her own intent. "I'm not doing this assignment," is probably *not* a defiant comment, but rather a statement of fact for this child. Further probing may reveal clues regarding the child's hesitancy to begin the assignment:

   • She doesn't know where to begin.

   • She doesn't understand what you want her to do.

   • She feels she can't complete the assignment without help.

   • She knows it will take her more time than she's been given.

   Reflect on all possible meanings, without rushing to conclusions. Be careful not to single her out in front of the class to try to make an example of her. This child will learn more acceptable verbal scripts if you make the effort to teach her appropriate verbal strategies which will allow her to modify her choice of words to convey her actual meaning.

4. **Observe and expand the coping techniques that the child has already acquired on her own.** Focus on developing flexible concepts and time order. Don't insist that this child conform to "normal" learning patterns; instead observe how she learns and try to utilize this method whenever introducing a new concept to her.

5. **Group this child with good role models so that she can label and learn appropriate social interaction.** Remember, left on her own, this child will not differentiate between appropriate versus inappropriate interactions. The distinctions need to be verbally pointed out to her. Sit her between mature, sensible classmates, so that she can establish good work habits. As often as possible, pair her with another student who enjoys helping this child and who is attentive to her needs. Since the child with NLD learns through verbalization, isolation is unacceptable for this child, as it will only exacerbate her problems.

6. **Adult role models should talk their way through decision-making situations in the presence of this child, in order to give her a verbal view of someone else's internal speech process.** In essence, you will be making your internal speech external, so that the child can learn how you evaluate a dilemma and hopefully procure the skills needed to develop her own decision-making approaches. Help the child devise a

sequence of steps for self-questioning and self-monitoring while verbalizing each step.

A five-step approach follows:

1. Define your issue. ("We're out of bread, but I don't have time to stop at the store before your ballet lesson.")

2. Verbalize some options you have. ("I could still stop at the store, but that would make us late. I could go back to the store while you have your lesson, but that would be back-tracking and a waste of time and gas. We could stop on the way back home, but that would mean we'd have a late dinner. Or, I could wait until tomorrow to get the bread, but you would have to buy your lunch at school tomorrow, because I won't have any bread for your sandwich.")

3. Try to determine your best option. ("I think I'll just have you buy your lunch tomorrow.")

4. Take that course of action. ("Put this money in your backpack now for your lunch tomorrow.")

5. Review your actions. Ask yourself if your plan proved effective. ("I think I chose the best option because I'm so short on time today. I had to change my original plan, but everything worked out. The next time I don't have time to get bread, I'll just have you buy your lunch at school the next day.")

There's a lot of self-talk that goes on in your head that you've probably never thought about. Whenever you make a decision, you talk yourself through it, albeit subconsciously. It's important for the child with NLD to continually hear these inner dialogues that are usually kept private, because she so often lacks the flexibility to weigh options (reason out), and falls apart when an obstacle to her normal routine presents itself. Learning the words that will connect what she does with a set procedure for decision-making allows this child to experience less anxiety when confronted with unexpected hurdles. Encourage her to approach problems verbally, using these five steps of analysis.

The long-range goal is to teach the child with NLD to use mental dialogue, or "self talk," for decision-making on her own by giving her a method to examine choices and plan ahead. This approach will produce more appropriate responses to the dilemmas she encounters. You want to encourage flexibility within a structured sequel. Because the five-step method illustrated here is sequential and analytical, the child is being taught to use left hemisphere functions to accomplish what others would know to do intuitively. (Be careful to limit the number of options in step 2, or the child will get bogged down and never move on from there.)

7. **Don't put additional or different expectations on this child before she has become comfortable with previous expectations.** When a child is doing well, it's natural to want to squeeze a little more out of her (the "strike while the iron's hot" school of philosophy). This can disrupt any previous progress made. The child with NLD is very slow to adapt to new input and new situations. Be sure she has been given an adequate amount of time to assimilate the old, before introducing any new expectations.

8. **Isolation, deprivation, and punishment are never effective methods to change the behavior of a child who is already trying her best to conform (but misinterpreting all kinds of nonverbal cues).** Avoid taking away an earned privilege as a punishment (example: a child with NLD wasn't allowed to participate in an ice-cream social she earned [by obtaining good grades and being on the "Principal's List"] because she fell out of her seat several times in class the morning of the social [owing to her NLD] — a highly unsuitable action on the part of her school staff.)

DEFINITION

BIP (Behavioral Intervention Plan)
a written plan for a child whose behavior significantly interferes with his learning and/or the other students' opportunities to learn, which specifically address those behaviors which interfere with learning. This plan must include a functional analysis of the child's behavior, as well as *nonpunitive* means for the child to acquire more acceptable replacement behaviors.

If inappropriate behaviors are causing problems at school, a functional analysis and Behavioral Intervention Plan (BIP) detailing a course of action which is designed to be useful and non-punitive in nature, may need to be a part of this child's IEP or 504 plan. Ostracizing and demoralizing a child is *never* an answer.

CAMS do not constitue lower or differential standards. The student with NLD is intellectually capable. By providing CAMS you are providing this child with the chance to profit from and demonstrate her level of intelligence.

Chapter 9
Helping the Child with NLD Acquire Social Skills

Many behaviorists believe that the symptoms of depression result from problems in interacting with other people . . .

Harley has always liked being around other people. But other people haven't always taken to Harley with the same enthusiasm. It's not that he isn't entertaining, it's just that Harley never seems to know when to let up. Even as a little tyke, he subjected his preschool friends to long monologues as though they were adults, and he verbally sparred with the adults in his life, as though they were his equals. Harley clearly never grasped the concept of pecking order. In fact, he argued with everyone so much, and so well, he was dubbed the "little attorney" at his preschool. Poor Harley . . . he just couldn't seem to figure out when enough was enough.

Harley's perceived argumentativeness continued in his early elementary years. He complained constantly about the unfair treatment he felt he received from his teachers. Finally, in fourth grade, Harley himself arranged a meeting with the school principal and his teachers (without his parents' knowledge). He was "fed up" and "wasn't going to take it anymore." Harley demanded his "perpetrators" attend and he eloquently stated his disapproval of the way things were being done at his school. When his math teacher failed to show up at the designated time, Harley took it upon himself to page the teacher over the school's intercom (without first securing permission from anyone). No one in the office could believe their eyes and ears. "How could this little kid have so much nerve?"

Harley didn't mean to be nervy; he was merely using his well-developed verbal mediation skills to try and make the world work for him. In addition to his unusual approach to social interactions, Harley was having difficulty completing written assignments and he displayed poor organizational skills at school. He qualified for the school's gifted program, but floundered in his regular fourth grade classroom. An intelligence screening revealed a VIQ of 159 and a PIQ of 122 (an extremely gifted child with a 37-point discrepancy between VIQ and PIQ!).

By fifth grade, Harley was complaining constantly to his parents that he couldn't keep up. An engineer and a nurse, his parents did everything they could to ease his suffering and to help him along. But when Christmas vacation came around, Harley refused to go back to school in January. He complained that he had no friends and that everyone picked on him. And, what's more, brilliant and engaging Harley, the "little attorney," couldn't figure out why his classmates and teachers shunned and castigated him . . . .

Remember, communication is comprised of both verbal and nonverbal modes of expression. Individuals with nonverbal learning disorders miss out on at least 65% of all communication, which is nonverbal. A child with NLD often does not have positive interactions with others because he lacks the social perception to elicit the desired feedback from them. Even so-called "verbal communication" is largely dependent upon extra-verbal pragmatic cues, such as:

- the tone in which a person's words are conveyed
- the pauses between words
- the way eye contact is shown
- the timing and pace of delivery

Social Skills — Learning the Untaught Code

The social ineptness of a child with NLD is *not* simply acquired from the learning disability because of issues of self-esteem which arise from the child's experiences of failure and the stigma which is attached to these experiences. There are fundamental, very distinguishing social deficits associated with NLD. This child will not learn or pick up from normal everyday situations the emotional and social information necessary to learn the rules necessary for appropriate social interaction. Things will happen right in front of him, and he will not notice what's going on, nor will he make sense of these occurrences. Nonverbal communication is a language this child doesn't have a code for, and rarely is this code directly taught to a child in our present-day society.

Social skills are comprised of an accumulation of subliminally learned (as opposed to directly taught) behaviors. Social competence comes from the effortless and intuitive use of these skills in everyday social situations. Early development of social skills is normally gleaned through imitation. Young children watch the behavior of those around them. They notice the subtle reactions of others to certain behaviors and form their own mental image of "appropriate" versus "inappropriate" conduct. In every culture, the most relevant aspects of social interaction are nonverbal.

The child with NLD is unable to perceive these unspoken laws of conduct which guide us in the acquisition of acceptable social skills. As a result, he exhibits a number of social incompetencies throughout his development, which are in no way deliberate on his part. He does not have access to the neurological processes which would allow him to cognitively develop exemplary behaviors through the observation of others. His attempts at socializing are routinely characterized by repetitive questioning and loquacious conversations. The effects of continually

124 *The Source for Nonverbal Learning Disorders*

misjudging what is going on can be devastating. Failing to read social cues, engaging in lengthy one-sided dialogues, and acting in a manner which is uncomfortable to others will eventually lead to social isolation and rejection.

Perceptions of Behavior Don't Reflect Reality

The unpredictable behaviors often exhibited by the child with NLD are usually misunderstood and misinterpreted by his peers and the adults in his life. The motivational force behind this child's behavior is the same as everyone else's: *he wants to be accepted and supported.* "Class clown" behavior can develop as an undesirable coping technique because the child with NLD does not want his classmates to know that he is unable to pick up on or do the things that they all accomplish without effort.

What teachers may dub as "excessive silliness" is a common behavioral presentation of a child with NLD. It usually starts with unintentional social blunders that are then repeated purposefully because the child realizes that he can make other children laugh. The reaction of the other children makes the child with NLD feel like he is a part of his peer group. The fact that his classmates are "laughing at him," and not "with him" isn't perceived. Although this child may have a high level of intelligence and good logical reasoning skills, he totally lacks decision-making and problem-solving skills. These skills will have to be directly taught to the child with NLD in a nonjudgmental fashion.

Since this child doesn't perceive situations holistically, he is often not aware of when he needs to modify what he says or does. This lack of social awareness can lead others to conclude that the child with NLD is boring, rude, too open, arrogant, or just plain argumentative. A number of his symptoms may resemble those of a behavior-disordered child, but it is actually his neurological deficits which are interfering with this child's ability to comply. Standard behavioral interventions don't work with the child with NLD. He has to be given specific guidelines and taught even the most simple social competencies, those that most children absorb without a second thought.

The social interactions of a child with NLD are often labeled and interpreted incorrectly. He might be seen as one or more of the following:
- *argumentative* — because he doesn't know when to stop talking
- *uncooperative* — because he insists on doing things a certain way
- *inattentive* — because he gets lost and is confused by directions
- *defiant* — because he is bright, but doesn't complete school assignments

- *disruptive* — because he knocks over objects, constantly drops things, falls out of seat, and talks out of turn
- *rude* — because talks back to adults
- *disrespectful* — because he uses an inappropriate tone of voice
- *boorish* — because he has difficulty conforming to social norms

None of these behaviors are enacted for "attention-getting" purposes and none of these descriptive labels are accurate.

By and large, the child with NLD rarely exhibits blatant behavioral problems. Nonetheless, the limitations of this child do create ongoing social interaction problems. Most children learn from their interactions with others and with their environment. But the child with NLD will focus on the symbolic details of his environment, rather than its more holistic cultural aspects. He doesn't discover the unspoken code of cause and effect through experience; this code needs to be pointed out to him intentionally and verbally.

How NLD Sabotages Social Skills

While other children are developing social competencies without much external guidance, through observation and imitation, the child with NLD requires constant verbal explanations to make sense of the things going on around him. He lacks insight into, and awareness of, the expectations of others. This child is unable to read body language, understand the use of body space, or pick up changes in voice tone and volume. The end result leads to difficulty socializing and interacting appropriately with other people. The child with NLD, throughout his development, displays a number of social incompetencies that should not be misinterpreted or dealt with as noncompliant behaviors.

Our perceptions of other people's feelings and emotions, as they are communicated through nonverbal forms of expression (gestures, inflection and intonation of voice, facial presentation, body posture, interpersonal space, etc.), serve as an important regulator of our own behavior. Subtle displays of variance reveal to us how we should react to another person. Studies have shown that the ability to "read" a mother's facial expression is well-developed in most infants by a few months of age. When placed in a novel situation, the normal infant will glance up at his mother's face, verify her facial expression, and respond accordingly. Fear in a mother's expression will cause the infant to become fearful, whereas a smile on the mother's face will cause the infant to relax and smile back. A blank expression on the mother's face will cause an infant to actually grow physically ill. He becomes anxious and confused because he can't read his mother's expression.

These studies help us to understand how the child with NLD feels most of the time, every day of his life — anxious and confused. He will experience marked feelings of helplessness throughout each day, related to his high level of anxiety. This child will react intensely to emotional, ambiguous, and novel events because he can't make sense of them; he can't take advantage of nonverbal prompts available to guide him. As a result, the child is easily overwhelmed and/or has difficulty distancing himself from these types of situations. He either avoids them altogether or becomes consumed by them. In short, the child with NLD can be a bundle of raw nerves, displaying a perplexing array of emotional reactions to the confusion he encounters. He has an enormous need for support, but his offensive behavior often results instead in disapproval and rejection. Sadly, because of the very nature of this disorder, this child is unable to communicate his need for support to others in a way they can respond to him with the empathy he deserves.

Throughout our lives, whenever we come across a mismatch, nonverbal communication is always given more credence than verbal communication (except in the case of a person with NLD). Imgaine two children playing on a playground. One of them starts shouting, his face turns red, and he is shaking all over.

"What are you so angry about?" the other child asks.

"Me? Angry?" the first child screams back. "I'm not angry!"

One message is being communicated verbally, while an entirely different message is conveyed through this child's nonverbal interaction. Is this boy angry (as his nonverbal reactions suggest)? Or isn't he angry (as his verbal response suggests)? Most people will conclude that the little boy with the red face *is* angry, regardless of his verbal denial.

Because nonverbal language is so much more dominant, serious conflicts arise for a child who fails to interpret another person's nonverbal forms of expression correctly, or for a child who sends out nonverbal messages that don't accurately convey his current emotions. If a person doesn't match his words with the correct gestures and postures, social interactions will be impaired and the person with these incompetencies will have no idea why this is happening or *even that it is happening*. The person with NLD goes through life taking in information based upon the meaning of the words spoken to him. He fails to comprehend that there are any other meanings being transmitted.

The child with NLD exhibits:
- difficulty projecting his own experiences to relate to those of another individual
- a lack of ability to intuit another person's feelings or to infer another person's intentions and beliefs
- an inability to recognize another person's emotions, unless these are verbally pointed out to him

When asked how a little boy in a picture (who had just fallen off his bike) might feel, Harley responded with, "How would I know?" Although his response may appear flippant on the surface, further examination reveals Harley's neurological inability to understand the world from a point of view outside of his own. Therefore, since he is not the boy in the picture, he doesn't know how that boy feels. His incompetency is made clear by then asking Harley if *he* has ever fallen off *his* bike and how he felt when that happened. Harley has no difficulty providing a detailed account of his own experiences. Please don't think that Harley is insensitive of others; he's not. Rather, he is "mind blind"; he can't see the world from other peoples' points of view.

Making and keeping friends is largely dependant upon a person's sensitivity to the needs and feelings of other people. The child with NLD has difficulty figuring out what someone else is thinking or how they are feeling, unless that person is giving him continuous verbal cues. Very few people do. Most communication, especially among close friends, is nonverbal. Our friends, the people we are most in sync with, are those whose nonverbal cues are most apparent to us. We avoid people who make us feel anxious, uneasy, uncomfortable, and/or afraid (those whose body language is vague or unreadable for us). The child with NLD is NOT asocial. He tries very hard to fit in with others. However, his attempts at developing friendships are continually frustrated by his own incompetencies. He is unable to attach meaning, comprehend, deal with, or respond internally and behaviorally to someone else's expressions and displays of emotion.

Change Is Not Good for the Child with NLD

The child with NLD will observe, memorize, and compile an overabundance of minute details regarding his environment, but will fail to form overall impressions (sees the trees, but not the forest syndrome). This leads to an inability to recognize similarities in new situations he encounters. Each new situation is perceived as a totally foreign experience for this child. His learning is contextual only; he lacks the ability to generalize from the vast amount of specific information he has stored. This makes it impossible to anticipate future events, so this child clings to the predictability of events which always stay the same. Extreme anxiety accompanies any changes. It is important to try and help this child to recognize the same information in different contexts.

Vacations can be pure hell for the child with NLD. He is suddenly thrown into a new situation, a new physical environment, a new sleeping arrangement, a new waking schedule, and he encounters a number of new people, all at the same time. Suddenly, there is no predictable structure to his day or his surroundings. The novel circumstances which provide excitement and fun for the rest of his family, torment the child with

128   *The Source for Nonverbal Learning Disorders*

NLD. Theme parks are generally too visually overstimulating for this child. He can build up an enormous amount of tension related to vacationing. This is in part because he can't visually coordinate what's going on around him and in part because he can't predict what will happen next. This child lacks the ability to anticipate and accommodate in novel surroundings. It seems to him that things are just happening without any logical order. Again, this sets up a scenario of tremendous fear and anxiety.

It is up to the adults in his life to help this child make sense of his confusing world by reducing the stress he encounters in his physical environment and by offering constant verbal explanations to him of everything that happens. The child with NLD responds well to clearly defined expectations and predictable outcomes. It is the unexpected and the unknown which scares, confuses, and threatens him, often resulting in puzzling behavioral reactions (such as Damon's refusal to participate in his birthday party and Harley's refusal to return to school after Christmas vacation). As much as possible, adults need to control the child's early social interactions, gradually relinquishing this control to him, as the child develops the competencies he needs to deal with the more complex situations in his life. Adaptability and flexibility need to be broached slowly and taught specifically.

This may mean that you need to hold off introducing a child to a novel situation (such as a noisy, crowded amusement park) or it may mean that you need to pre-plan to avoid causing a difficult adjustment for your child (such as limiting the number of children present at a birthday party). Assemblies and field trips are often difficult for the child with NLD because of the newness of the situation. As we have seen, family vacations can be catastrophic.

Preparing for Change

It may be necessary to limit novel experiences such as field trips, visits to theme parks, and surprise parties. Whenever possible, pre-plan and prepare well in advance. And, involve your child with NLD in the planning stages so that he has as much advance readiness as possible. Once you see that your child has built some effective coping strategies, then try re-introducing experiences you've eliminated, being constantly alert to your child's response to these circumstances.

Remember Damon's reaction to his surprise birthday party at the beginning of Chapter 1? He was confused and frightened, and refused to come out and enjoy himself. If you place a child with NLD, unprepared, into a novel and visually stimulating situation like a birthday party where there is a multitude of colors, lights, decorations, and children running about, his mind will automatically switch to overload. He can't decipher what is relevant in this situation and he, therefore, can't accommodate to the novelty of the situation. Advance preparation is critical.

After Damon's disastrous surprise party, the next year his mother began planning his birthday party several months ahead of time, and Damon participated in the preparations every step of the way. He went with his mother to select and purchase the decorations and party favors, choosing each item himself. Then, Damon decided where the decorations would go in his house. They were put up gradually, over a period of several days, so that Damon could get used to each change. He picked out his cake design himself from samples displayed at the bakery.

And, Damon decided who he would invite (two friends and a couple of relatives) and hand-delivered the invitations (which he had designed on his computer). The day before the actual party, his parents staged a rehearsal, going through everything they anticipated would happen. For most children, this type of approach would cause the party itself to be anticlimactic. However, with Damon, systematically preparing him in advance made all the difference. This time Damon really enjoyed his party and all future novel situations were approached by his parents in this same methodical manner.

When Harley's mother received a notice that his fourth-grade class would be going on a field trip to the zoo, she wondered if she should keep Harley home that day. He loved animals, but his track record on field trips was poor. In fact, his teacher had threatened to exclude Harley from all future field trips if he didn't "shape up" this time. Harley said he didn't care. Field trips were just a hassle anyway. He would rather stay at school and do his reading and spelling.

Harley's mother had another plan. She got the agenda from Harley's teacher and previewed it with Harley. Then she took Harley, the weekend before the class trip, to all the sites his class intended to visit at the zoo. She made comments at each location and gave Harley verbal cues that he could fall back on when he was on his own. This helped ease Harley's reluctance considerably on the day of the actual field trip, but it didn't prevent him from becoming lost from the group and being teased by the other children. (His mother would have preferred to accompany the class, but she couldn't rearrange her work schedule.) It should have been the teacher's responsibility to try to ward off the possibilities of Harley getting lost and being teased. Still, the day certainly went better for Harley than some of his past experiences, owing to his mother's diligence in preparing him ahead of time.

The Source for Nonverbal Learning Disorders

The Naive World of NLD

As was discussed earlier, the child with NLD often fails to understand the motivations and intentions of others. He interprets everything in its most literal context. Inferences are missed. This child may find it difficult to share in a casual social dialogue. Long-winded, one-sided conversations often ensue. Like Katie, this child may become overly distressed

by teasing and sarcasm, exhibiting a low level of tolerance for frustration and failure. And, as we've seen with Harley, although he may want very much to meet new people and develop friendships, his efforts are constantly thwarted by awkward approaches and a failure to read the nonverbal communication of others. This child isn't lacking in desire, but rather he lacks the skills necessary to successfully engage the interest of others. Speech and language therapy can be helpful in fostering conversational skills. The following areas of language pragmatics should be stressed:

- turn-taking
- sensitivity to cues provided by the other person
- typical rules of conversation

The child with NLD does not intuitively understand the concept of lying and therefore doesn't question or evaluate the information he receives from others. This leaves him defenseless against the deception and mockery of the more cunning individuals he encounters. Complex social interactions, such as persuasion, negotiation, and resisting peer pressure, are often beyond his scope of cognizance. He is the one egged on by more street-wise children. This child is extremely vulnerable and requires diligent protection from playground bullies and unscrupulous strangers (as we've seen illustrated in the examples of Joseph, Colton, Mallory and all the others).

The child with NLD himself is honest to a fault, which is also not always appreciated by those in authority (i.e. adult complains: "He readily admitted what he'd done, showing no remorse or apprehension." or "Can you believe the nerve? This kid just walked right up and told me my perfume stinks!"). Although this child may appear callous or rude, adults need to understand that he is really doing the best he can with what he knows. The child with NLD needs to be helped, not condemned. If this child is constantly being told he is "bad" or "rude," given his black-and-white perception of right and wrong, his already fragile sense of self-esteem will only be further diminished.

Providing a Positive Influence

The constant reminders that he is failing to conform socially can only have a negative impact upon both this child's growth and self-esteem. All learning occurs more readily when a child has positive relationships with adults, as well as peers — when he feels he belongs. Many behaviorists believe that the symptoms of depression result from problems in interacting with other people. Serious problems with self-esteem eventually develop in almost all children with NLD because of their contradictory relationships with others. This child learns to have little confidence in himself, as his social blunders continue to plague him. His unintentional, "annoying" behaviors inundate him with negative feedback and they may eventually be the cause of social rejection (as we have seen with Harley) and deep-seated feelings of helplessness.

When a child's best efforts continuously fail to meet the expectations of those around him, his repeated failures, and the constant criticism he receives, erode at his self-esteem. Then the child feels totally defeated and unworthy of anyone's praise. As more acceptable behaviors are verbally pointed out to him, the child with NLD will gain a better understanding of the subtle interactions going on around him, and better understand what is expected of him in social situations. And, as he begins to gain more social competencies, he will become less anxious, more flexible, and more at ease in social situations.

Remembering that NLD is a neurological disorder, and not a behavioral disorder, is crucial in helping this child acquire more desirable social behaviors. Behavior modification systems and programs are all based upon the assumption that the child knows how to behave appropriately and merely requires motivations to help him "remember" or sanctions (punishments) to discourage him when he does not comply. In the case of the child with NLD, these assumptions are totally invalid. A behavior modification program can only serve to create increased anxiety for this child and should be avoided. The changes in social behavior you seek will come about through the acquisition of social competencies, directly and deliberately taught.

Most adult displays of approval and disapproval rely largely upon the use of nonverbal social reinforcers — tone of voice (as in calling out the child's name in a particular way), pat on the back, swat on the behind, giving extra attention, ignoring, smiling, frowning, touching, avoiding, spending extra time with or separating from the child are all intended to communicate a specific message to that child about his recent actions. The child with NLD doesn't respond appropriately to the tone of voice and facial characteristics of others. All nonverbal parental social reinforcers should be accompanied by descriptive words of praise or nonjudgmental explanations of your displeasure in order to impart meaning to the child with NLD. Nonverbal social reinforcers should only be given *along with* descriptive words, if they are to be effective.

132 *The Source for Nonverbal Learning Disorders*

Building Social Skills

Following are some suggestions which have been specifically tailored for the child with NLD to assist in the development of appropriate social skills:

1. **Teach social skills verbally.**

   Reasons, rules and reminders help the child with NLD learn *when* he is expected to do *what*, since he isn't accruing the visual and nonverbal cues which help teach the rest of us social protocol. Verbally discuss and model for him the common unwritten rules of social interaction and the reasons behind them. Remember, this child will not pick up nonverbal messages from his environment the way other children do. But he can be taught rules of behavior in a very defined manner. Tell your child specifically what "appropriate" behaviors are, how he can achieve them, and why they are necessary. Terms like *being good*, *being polite*, *minding*, etc., are all abstract concepts which need to be broken down into their specific components. State all rules concretely and positively. Repeat rules as often as necessary.

   When you spell out specific rules to the child with NLD, social interaction becomes easier for him. Abstract social concepts such as *cooperation, consideration, responsibility,* and *respect,* all need to be more clearly defined. To be of value to this child, rules need to be concise, stated positively, and easy to memorize. There should be a reason for the rule and a condition under which the rule is applicable. These rules will help your child figure out what is expected of him.

   Instead of saying, "You will get in trouble if you don't obey me!" (which is not only negatively phrased, but the words *get in trouble* and *obey* are also highly abstract and threatening), start simply with, "You need to get into your bed when I tell you because that means it's time for you to sleep." This phrasing also specifies the conditions under which the rule is applicable — "when I tell you." Another example of a simply stated explicit rule is, "Do not cross the street when the light says 'Don't Walk' because that means a car could be coming."

   The child with NLD may ask for a more detailed explanation, but he probably will not quibble about getting into bed when told or not crossing the street when the sign says "Don't Walk"; he likes rules that are concrete and that he can quickly and easily memorize. In fact, *what his logical, linear brain really wants is a rule and a reason for everything.* He will probably not apply this rule to other similar situations, and he may have to be verbally reminded when the situation occurs again, but you will have a positive start to build from.

It is important to give reasons when you are stating rules to the child with NLD. The left brain is very logical and responds well to *specific* reasoning, as opposed to ubiquitous statements such as "Because I said so!" or "That's just the way it is!" There is a danger, if you use this type of unrestricted reasoning, that the child will come to believe that he should do whatever anybody tells him to do, which is certainly not your intent in defining rules. When the child is still quite young, you can begin having him repeat back the reasons and conditions for a particular rule. For example:

> Parent: Why do we have to wait here until the light changes?
>
> Child: Because when the sign says "Don't Walk" a car could be coming.

After your child answers the question correctly, rephrase your rule and say the whole thing back to him. He can start to see that there are different ways to say the same thing.

> Parent: Yes, we wait on the sidewalk until the light displays the word 'Walk' to be sure we don't step out in front of a car.

When your child is able to tell you the reasons for specific rules of behavior, begin to work on more general rules. Generalizations will probably prove to be difficult for the child with NLD to assimilate. Even when your child is able to cognitively describe what is expected of him, he is still often unable to act upon his knowledge in an intuitive and spontaneous fashion or to apply a specific rule to another similar situation. You may find that he sometimes relies upon formal rules of behavior in an almost rigid, unnatural fashion.

General (more abstract) rules about behavior are taught by pointing out the relationship between a specific rule and a more universal rule. An example of adding a generalization follows:

> Parent: You wait on the sidewalk when the light displays the words 'Don't Walk' because a car might be coming. *When you read and obey traffic signs, you will be safer.*

Continually point out social information to your child every time you encounter a situation, every place you go. Every meal, every trip in the car, every visit to the store, every family gathering . . . never miss an opportunity to teach him social awareness. The child with NLD isn't learning about the world around him unless you are talking to him.

Get used to well-meaning friends, relatives, and even teachers who inform you, "You don't have to tell him every little thing! Let him figure it out for himself . . . ." Ignore them. *You do have to tell your child with NLD every little thing* because that's how he will learn. The child's strong verbal skills should always be used as the primary means of developing appropriate and safe social behavior.

2. **Preview and prepare for new situations.**

   Whenever possible, preview and prepare for new situations before they arise. Feelings of insecurity and displays of social incompetence can result from ventures into unfamiliar territory. Try to always verbally prepare your child for changes or new experiences before they take place. Talking about the event ahead of time gives the child a chance to prepare for what is to come (don't wait until the visual-spatial confusion of a new or novel situation overwhelms your child to try to discuss what's going on). Preview, prepare, and explain — explain what you expect to happen, explain who will be involved, and explain how your child might best handle possible scenarios. This process provides a foundation of support for him to refer back to throughout his new encounter.

   Example:
   You are going to Aunt Jane's house for the first time. Explain to your child that Aunt Jane has some slightly different rules at her house and specify in detail what they are. ("She doesn't allow children in her living room" or "She expects people to take their shoes off before walking on her carpet.") Also talk about guest behavior and how it differs from acceptable behavior within your own home ("You must ask Aunt Jane before turning on her TV or going into her refrigerator."). This child will not watch the others around him to determine appropriate behavior. Give the child with NLD as many verbal cues as you can ahead of time. Also, if there are topics of discussion that are better left unsaid, tell your child before you arrive ("Aunt Jane has a large purple scar on her forehead that she doesn't like to talk about, so we have to be careful not to mention it.").

   The child with NLD won't observe differences in protocol the way other children do. You need to *spell out everything* to him. Advance preparation will help avoid a lot of embarrassing social blunders for your child. Because this child stores information through rote memory rather than through concept formation, he often says things that other people barely dare to think. His intentions are usually misunderstood by the victims of these unwitting remarks. Get in the habit of pre-discussing everything, long after you think it "should be" necessary. The child with NLD wants to be accepted and to interact appropriately in social situations. And, he can achieve successes with advance preparation.

3. **Always validate your child after a social blunder.**
   It's obviously impossible to preview and prepare for *every* situation ahead of time. Difficult situations for your child that you didn't anticipate will undoubtedly occur. Discuss these incidents as they arise and verbally offer an alternative behavior or reaction to your child. But, be careful *not* to do this in a reprimanding fashion. Don't tell him what he did wrong; instead teach him what he should do the next time. A good approach to keep in mind is to always validate the child's previous action before offering him a more appropriate alternative. Here are two examples:

   > "*I know you didn't mean* to hurt Ashley's feelings when you said 'I don't want to play with you because you're boring.' But, next time you could simply say, 'I need to do something else right now.' That way, Ashley doesn't end up with hurt feelings."

   > "*I know you didn't realize* that walking away when Coach Bowen was talking to you would upset him, but next time, even if you think you know what he is going to say, wait until he has finished talking before walking away. This is a courtesy children must show to adults who are helping them."

   Be clear and concise and *don't place blame* on the child for his lack of social skills.

4. **Help this child decipher meanings.**
   Although the child with NLD talks a lot, he may have difficulty deciphering the abstract meanings of normal conversation. This child has trouble using his well-developed language as a tool for social interaction. While he is highly capable of talking *at* people, his misses a lot of the inferences and the many abstract subtleties of our language. Help your young child with NLD learn expected responses to common questions that are abstract in nature by explaining the intent of the question and modeling appropriate answers. Here are some examples of explanations:

   > "How are you?" generally means "How are you feeling today?" If you feel fine, say, "I'm fine." But, if you feel sick, you would say, "I don't feel so good."

   > "Are you ready?" generally means "Do you have everything you need for the next activity? Could you do it right now?" If you have everything you need, say, "Yes, I'm ready." But, if you need more time, you would say, "No, I'm not quite ready."

 The Source for Nonverbal Learning Disorders

By previewing possible responses with your child, he not only learns to cope with some of the abstract subtleties of our language, but he also learns some appropriate interactive social skills as well. When watching television or reading stories with your child, take the time to point out non-literal use of language and explain the motives behind people's actions. This is also a good time to discuss the social behavior of the characters, explaining appropriate versus inappropriate behaviors and reactions.

5. **Avoid abstract responses to your child's behavior.**
   When you praise your child, describe in clear verbal terms what he has done that pleases you. Likewise, when your child displays inappropriate behavior, be descriptive and nonjudgmental in your responses to him. Try to avoid abstract phrasing.

   Positive nonverbal social reinforcers such as smiling, winking, nodding, clapping, hugging, stroking, patting, etc., should only be given *along with* descriptive words of praise such as, "You wrote your name very neatly on your paper. I know that took you a lot of time. I'm so proud of you. You did a nice job!" or "You remembered to wait for your brother to finish talking before you told me about your video game. I know it was hard for you to wait. I'm glad you were considerate of your brother. That was a good boy." This method of offering praise always clearly defines, in specific verbal terms, the action you are reinforcing and, at the same time, you can take advantage of the opportunity to demonstrate an appropriate nonverbal social reinforcer to go along with your words of praise.

   A lot of confusion for the child is eliminated by using descriptive terms of praise, rather than just generalized abstract statements such as, "You did a nice job!" or "That was a good boy." By providing clear and explicit examples of the behaviors you are praising in the beginning, you are defining components of the more general abstract concepts that the child with NLD is often unable to comprehend initially, such as doing a *nice job*, being a *good boy*, being *considerate, cooperating, obeying, minding, showing respect for others*, etc.

   Explanations of inappropriate behaviors should also be descriptive and nonjudgmental. Validate the child first, before describing to him what he should have done differently. Here are two examples:

   "I know you didn't mean to be inconsiderate of your brother when you came up and started telling me about your video game. But he was talking to me first and you should have let him finish. I hope you will remember this next time. When someone else is talking, wait for that person to finish before you begin talking."

"I know you would never hurt our computer on purpose. But when you spilled your chocolate milk on the keyboard, that gummed up the keys. I've told you before to keep food and drinks away from the computer. When you need a snack break, keep your food and drinks in the kitchen."

This method of explaining always *validates the child first* and then clearly defines, in specific verbal terms, the action you seek to eliminate, without placing blame on the child for his unintentional negligence. Keep in mind that a lot of the confusion this child experiences can be eliminated if you remember to use descriptive terms, rather than just abstract statements, which personally attack the child, such as, "You misbehaved today!" or "That was a bad boy!"

6. **Do not use ultimatums.**
    Try to avoid "if you _____ , then _____ will happen to you" ultimatums because this places pressure upon the child to perform in situations where he may not be capable of responding in an appropriate manner, *even* when your intent was to establish a positive outcome. Here's an example of a seemingly positive ultimatum:

    "If you say only nice things to Grandma, then I'll give you one of your favorite cookies when we get home."

This ultimatum unwittingly sets up fear, confusion and anxiety for the child with NLD because he wants the cookie, but he doesn't know what you mean by "nice things." The child may ask for a definition of "nice things" and be told, "things that don't hurt her feelings." This inexplicit answer creates even more frustration because the child doesn't know *what things hurt her feelings.* It's better to be specific, as in:

    "Be sure to tell Grandma how attractive her garden looks. This will make her happy. But, we won't mention any scraggly plants we see because Grandma works hard in her garden and we don't want to upset her."

Don't attach any ultimatums, but be sure to verbally praise your child afterward for *remembering*.

Even worse than straightforward ultimatums are negatively phrased if-then threats such as on the following page.

138 *The Source for Nonverbal Learning Disorders*

"If you don't behave at grocery store this morning, then you can't go to the baseball game this afternoon."

This will undoubtedly induce fear, confusion and anxiety for the child with NLD because he wants to go to the ball game, but he isn't sure what you mean by "behaving" at the grocery store. Instead of producing the result you desired (appropriate behavior), you are more likely to elicit the opposite outcome (inconsistent behavior), because the child's anxiety (worrying about missing the ball game) has mounted to the point where he is completely unable to concentrate on the task at hand. The child who is continually threatened in this manner begins to avoid those situations where his incompetencies may cause social errors, rather than learning a set of skills which will help him to become more competent in those situations. As a general principle, eliminate if-then ultimatums as a functional reinforcement approach.

7. **Don't abandon your child to sink or swim.**
   Do not leave your child on his own in complex social situations, such as scout groups or team sport activities, for which he is unprepared. Remember not to be in a rush to force independence and self-responsibility on this child. Be especially careful not to compare him with other children his same age. In all new activities, let him get his feet wet gradually, at his own pace. It is detrimental to socially isolate him, but don't err in the opposite direction by making the mistake of thinking he can be left totally on his own when faced with new or complex situations. Let him feel safe and successful in a controlled environment before leaving him to his own devices. Prepare your child for the situation and carefully plan the situation for your child. Here are some specific pointers to remember:

   • It is better to invite one friend over to play a number of times before you allow two or three children to invade your child's security. The child with NLD is overwhelmed by too many variables.

   • Parents may need to facilitate friendships, at first, by providing supervised outings and structured play situations.

   • Use your child's special interests and talents to prompt his participation in social activities.

   • Age-appropriate board games and games with well-defined rules can help ease the transition from isolated play to interactive social play.

   • Gradually increase the length of planned play sessions, as you see positive responses from your child.

- Individual sports, such as swimming and skiing, can be noncompetitive and fun to take part in with others (and prove much more beneficial than team sports where the emphasis is often placed on winning or losing).
- The focus of all activities should be on participation, enjoyment, and a personal sense of accomplishment.

When your child starts school, be sure to invite children from his class home to play. These play sessions should be short and very structured in the beginning. Monitor their activities and watch closely for teasing and bullying and other children taking advantage of your child. Allow more latitude as you see your child successfully handling these situations. Group social situations can then be considered. Avoid loud, boisterous, disorderly groups with no clear structure. Explain your child's needs and limitations to his scout leader or coach. If this person is not receptive, seek another situation for group interaction. A proactive approach is always preferable to a reactive approach.

As he matures, the child with NLD will probably gravitate toward special interest groups such as a computer club, a school or church choir, or a debate club, rather than more open-ended, less-structured, groups such as the Boy Scouts, youth recreation groups, or sports teams. Try to ensure his success in as many circumstances as possible. Always strive to prepare your child in advance and to give him the verbal compensatory strategies he will need to deal more effectively with life's novel situations. Talk about the skills everyone needs to learn in order to function as part of a group. Your goal should be to reduce the stress your child encounters on a daily basis in his physical surroundings, while at the same time helping him to become more competent and adaptable interacting in society.

8. **Incentives don't work.**
   Remember, you can't correct social incompetencies resulting from a neurological disorder with stars, stickers, points, poker chips, charts, rewards, or prizes. This approach assumes a lack of motivation to be the cause of the behaviors you seek to eliminate. If this were the case, it would make sense to add a little additional incentive for the child. However, the child with NLD is probably already working at over 100% of his capacity, trying to conform to confusing standards, despite his lack of access to his right-hemisphere functions.

   This child's underlying deficiencies will not go away just because you try to make his positive behaviors more rewarding for him. All this will do is to intensify his frustration when he falls short of your expectations. Unrealistic expectations only exacerbate the feelings of inadequacy and worthlessness your child may already be experiencing. *When his brain is under too much stress from the environment, he is more likely to act out than to comply.* Please don't compare his behavior to that of other children his age. Assume he needs direct intervention and guidance, not motivational ploys and certainly not punishments. (Always avoid the use of punishment to try to correct behavior resulting from a neurological deficit. Even greater problems can be created when punishment is used in this way.)

Please note, like all children, the child with NLD thrives upon your recognition and reinforcement of his efforts. Condition your approach around praising and making sure your feedback is free of negative judgments. *Praise and reward this child often for his accomplishments; just be careful that you don't make the mistake of setting up a token economy reinforcement system or any other type of behavioral program that is contingent upon the child's performance to secure your approval (i.e., if the child performs in the way you desire, he earns your favor; if not, reinforcement is denied).* Always allow your child the dignity and respect he deserves. He is not a "bad" child; he just needs a little extra help and guidance to learn the social behavior that most children grasp intuitively.

9. **Don't ignore socially inappropriate behavior.**
   Differential reinforcement or ignoring is also not advised. Ignoring behavior that is unacceptable (based upon the assumption that the child undertakes it for attention-seeking purposes) doesn't give the child with NLD the verbal input he requires to develop the skills to behave in a more appropriate manner in future situations. Ignoring is a very nonverbal way of communicating to a child that you're not pleased with a particular action or statement. The child with NLD will not pick up on this message, even if positive reinforcement is given for more acceptable behaviors.

   We all know that constructive behavioral changes in children will result from the use of praise and that negative outcomes can be expected from the use of criticism. With most children, differential reinforcement (giving no reinforcement to undesired behaviors) will, in time, also produce positive behavioral changes. However, ignoring the social blunders of the child with NLD doesn't allow this child to receive the verbal feedback he needs in order to understand the effect of his behavior upon others. Tell him specifically what is acceptable and unacceptable. A common response from a child with NLD who is being scolded for inappropriate behavior is, "You never *told* me not to do this." Don't reprimand him, and certainly don't criticize him, *but do talk to him.* Explain more acceptable behavior to him in a nonjudgmental way.

10. Consider social skills training groups.

Social skills training groups may be useful, at some point, if there are adequate opportunities during the group session for your child to practice specific skills with the therapist and, if you, as parents, are trained to follow-through with the specific techniques and strategies in your home environment.

The Yale/LDA Social Learning Disabilities Study outlines the following goals for Social Skills Training:

- appropriate nonverbal communicative behavior (use of gaze, inflection of voice, body space, etc.)

- verbal decoding of the nonverbal behaviors of others

- processing of visual information simultaneously with auditory information (to facilitate the creation of appropriate social context)

- social awareness, perspective-taking skills, and correct interpretation of ambiguous communications (nonliteral language)

Social skills training groups which seek to decrease social incompetencies through behavioral modification programs aren't geared for the child with NLD.

11. Consider professional counseling.

If your child, through continuous failures in his interactions with others, has withdrawn and avoids social interactions (such as we've seen happen to both Joseph and Harley), professional counseling can help and should be considered. (Again, you will need to make sure the professional you choose has a clear understanding that your child's social incompetencies stem from a specific neurological basis and that this person designs his or her approach to your child with this in mind).

The focus should be on practical, directive-type therapies, not insight-oriented, nondirective, psycho-dynamic type therapies. The therapist should assume a positive coaching role. One of the goals should be to help your child better understand his limitations and also to aid him in self-acceptance through self-advocacy skills.

Chapter 10
Transitioning Toward Adulthood

Every parent's goal is to help his or her child develop into a competent adult able to function independently in the outside world . . .

Hollyanne's parents recognized early on that their daughter had a unique way of interacting with the world. But they never anticipated the difficulties Hollyanne would encounter once she started school.

"We always knew Hollyanne was bright because she was an early talker and taught herself to read before she started school. I guess that's why it was so hard for us to understand how she could face so many trials and tribulations at school," Hollyanne's mother laments now. "From day one, Hollyanne seemed confused and defenseless — like a fish out of water. If only we knew then what we know now . . . ."

Hollyanne was first pegged a "behavior problem" in kindergarten, and her run-ins with school authorities compounded during her elementary years, until she finally bottomed-out in middle school. She always seemed to "be in the wrong place, at the wrong time, doing the wrong thing." Academic obstacles centered around her failure to complete assignments and her difficulties with handwriting. Because Hollyanne received failing grades in several of her classes during her eighth grade year, her mother enrolled her in a small, private alternative high school, believing Hollyanne just needed a different approach to learning.

Even though Hollyanne resisted the change in environment, she eventually learned to get along well with the small class sizes and with all of her classes located in one building. Written assignments were modified for her because of her obvious difficulties holding a pencil and getting her thoughts on paper. And, Hollyanne's parents spent hours each night helping her keep up with her school work. Subsequently, Hollyanne's grades shot back up, along with her self-esteem.

For her junior year of high school, at age 16, Hollyanne had been doing so well at the private school, that she re-enrolled at her public high school. She took the PSAT in preparation for college applications. That was when her school counselor sat up and took notice. Her achievement in the verbal areas was at the 98th percentile, while the nonverbal areas scored at the 21st percentile.

The marked discrepancy between these scores prompted him to initiate a request for a special education assessment battery. A 22-point discrepancy between her VIQ and PIQ was revealed. This profile, in combination with her early school history, fit the criteria for a diagnosis of NLD.

ITP (Individualized Transition Plan)
The specific transition plan and strategies required for a student who is 16 years of age or older, who qualifies for special education services under PL92-142 (IDEA). The ITP contains a plan for the successful transition of the student from school to work, additional training or higher education, and community living.

For the first time, everyone looked at Hollyanne's difficulties in a new light. An IEP and an ITP were developed and implemented. Hollyanne remained fully included at her regular public high school.

The Goals of Education

Each child's schooling should be viewed as a journey with a specific beginning and an ultimate destination. In order for a child to move toward a successful adult life, it is necessary to maximize her potential while she is still in school. The aim of all education programs should be that, upon completion, the child will be prepared for the following:

- involvement in her community
- participation in social activities with friends
- to be a contributing adult member of our society.

In other words, the goal of all childhood educational programs is to enhance the pursuit of a meaningful adult life.

These goals do not change because of the presence of a neurological disorder. Basic educational goals should be the same for everyone. Although the fundamental objectives for every child attending school are the same, the approach to arrive at a successful outcome will vary. An Individualized Educational Program and an Individualized Transitional Program should define the educational road map for a teenager with NLD.

With her IEP and ITP now in place, at age 18, Hollyanne has maintained a 3.0 grade average. She has her own checking account (which she manages and balances herself), has been driving a car for two years (with only a few minor mishaps), and she maintains an afternoon job as a teller at a local bank (in connection with her high school's "workability" program). She will graduate with her classmates in June and plans to go on to college. After all of their struggles getting her through school, Hollyanne's parents feel they can finally see the light at the end of the tunnel as they watch their daughter slowly, but surely, transitioning successfully toward adulthood.

Letting Go of a Child with NLD

Every parent's goal is to help his or her child develop into a competent adult able to function independently in the world. As your child with NLD emerges from adolescence, and the transition from childhood to adulthood begins to take place, a whole new set of challenges arise. This passage from child to adult, from schoolroom to workplace, and from dependence to independence is a gradual process, but one which must be monitored vigilantly by both parents and educators. Luckily, there are some specific steps parents and educators can take in order to help prepare the child with NLD for this process of transition.

It is crucial to remember that a child does not "outgrow" NLD. Hopefully, she has perfected a number of compensatory strategies and has survived the limitations of her neurological dysfunction thus far. This then, becomes the age at which it is imperative that your child with NLD begin to develop some self-advocacy survival skills. Upon exiting high school, she will need to be able to advocate for herself, in order to continue her successes. Having said this, I will concede that, in real life, this is much easier said than done! Parents and teachers can help facilitate this process by modeling the skills needed for self-advocacy and providing some of the tools this child will need to succeed. No one is empowered without help, support, and understanding. It is a lengthy process.

Coping skills and tools for self-advocacy are the two essential keys to a successful transition to adulthood. Once Hollyanne's NLD was diagnosed, her parents were able to view her future more realistically. They found out about accommodations that would be available for her on various college campuses (early registration, priority scheduling, note-takers, extended time, special test areas, modified written assignments, etc.) and they also researched on-the-job accommodations that would make successful employment possible for Hollyanne (please see Chapter 11 for a list of common stumbling blocks in the workplace and appropriate CAMS to circumvent them).

NLD and Adolescence

The last thing a teenager wants is to feel disconnected from her peer group. As an individual matures, concerns over peer judgement and peer alliance heighten. The feelings of isolation and segregation which often occur because of a learning disorder can become especially humiliating during the teen years. In addition to dealing with the everyday problems which arise from NLD, the teenager is also trying to separate from her parents and family and to develop a life of her own. The desire to be viewed as an individual in her own right is paramount. It is only natural for her to desire to be independent, self-reliant, self-sufficient, and autonomously competent. This need, coupled with the increased academic demands of high school, combine to make the transition period an especially difficult time to cope. The individual with NLD can easily become overwhelmed, but she may be too inundated to understand or admit it. Discreet support of this child is still needed.

Her parents now know that Hollyanne will always be hesitant to enter new situations. She will need previews and time to prepare herself for changes. Hollyanne is comfortable with her present routine because it is highly predictable. But her elementary school years are looked back upon as a nightmare, one she doesn't want to see repeated, ever. It is difficult, even now, for her to understand why the adults she counted on, and the children she sought out as friends, rejected and ridiculed her. And, she still has difficulties developing close personal relationships. Hollyanne lacks spontaneity, and will never be a social butterfly, but she does have one best friend that she has become quite close to during her last two years of high school.

A Realistic Future

Hollyanne plans to attend the same junior college as her friend, Melissa. This is an excellent idea because Melissa can act as her mentor and help ease the stress of passage from high school to college for Hollyanne. Hollyanne has a logical understanding now of what it means to have nonverbal learning disorders. She knows and can verbalize that she has to do things differently from most other people because she can't access a part of her brain which is available to most others. And, she knows that everything takes her much longer than her peers. But Hollyanne has also learned a number of successful coping techniques to help her deal with the confusion she encounters on a daily basis.

Although Hollyanne still doesn't see the whole picture when she is processing verbal information, she now recognizes that there is more to communication than exactly what she hears. She has learned to ask, "Are you being sarcastic?" or "Are you serious?" or "Is that a question that isn't really a question?" to try to make sense out of her interactions with others, when she becomes confused. As she prepares to head off to college, Hollyanne has clearly come a long way from the horrible days she spent sitting in the principal's office wondering what she'd said or done wrong. She plans to expand her strong computer skills and seek employment related to these skills. Hollyanne, at last, has a positive outlook for the future.

"Now, instead of that helpless little fish out of water, I see Hollyanne as a determined little fish, always struggling to swim upstream," her mother confided in me recently. "She's in the swim of things . . . but she still has to work so much harder than everyone else just to remain afloat! I'm so grateful that she's making progress. That's all we can ask."

The growing years of a child with NLD require constant vigilance on the part of her parents to ensure that their child is not discriminated against. Just because this child reaches a certain age, does not automatically mean she is ready to fend for herself. I feel strongly that there is a niche for everyone in the world, and that certainly includes the individual with NLD. It is absolutely critical, however, that this individual find just the right fit in college or career choices, allowing her to make the best of her abilities and progress toward a fulfilling life. The challenge for parents and educators is to help this child reach the point where she can find her niche and to prepare her to experience success when she does. It is important that the child with NLD be provided with compensatory strategies while still in school, so that she can successfully make the transition from school to work, additional training or higher education, or living in the community on their own. The goals of parents and educators should be the same.

Suggestions for Transitioning

If an individual has NLD, it is essential that she understand what this means and the impact that it has upon her school, family, and social life. She must understand which things are more difficult for her and how she can compensate for and accommodate these problems and situations as they arise. Without this awareness, she will not be successful in advocating for herself when she is on her own. The ultimate goal is for the adult to function independently in the outside world. Following are some suggestions to keep in mind during the transitionary period:

1. **Overcoming Resistance in High School**

   The most significant problem an individual with NLD is likely to encounter in high school is resistance from teachers and peers. Although this student is legally entitled to CAMS, that doesn't always mean they will automatically be implemented without protest or suspicion. Teachers may doubt the need for accommodations because the student's neurological condition is invisible and because the student appears so competent. And, her peers may feel bilked because they presume that more is being required of them than the student receiving CAMS.

   Education is the best vehicle for both of these groups. A good IEP will include provisions for staff inservice training. The individual with NLD should *not* be expected to run her own interference. Enlist the aid of a skilled and knowledgeable counselor or administrator. It's *their job* to ensure that IEPs are properly implemented (not the student's)! Also, when encountering resistance at the high school level, it's a good idea to keep in mind that college level professors and students tend to be much better equipped to deal with all manner of disabilities and much more tolerant of individuals with learning differences.

2. Preparing to Leave Home

Leaving home is a major life change. As with any transition, approach it in increments. The tremendous adjustments of independent living require continued support from parents and friends. A gradual introduction of practical life skills prior to leaving home will help the individual with NLD prepare for independence. Before attempting to do it on her own, the young adult with NLD should have had extensive experience with everyday functional activities, such as driving a car or negotiating public transportation, balancing her own checkbook, developing and sticking to a budget, doing laundry, and preparing basic meals.

3. Know Your Rights

Before leaving high school, an individual's diagnosis should be confirmed or reaffirmed (make certain assessment data is up-to-date). There are distinct entitlements that go along with the diagnosis of NLD. These are rights that are guaranteed to any person with a disability living in the United States. Under Section 504 of the Rehabilitation Act of 1973, a college student has rights to reasonable accommodations corresponding to her specific needs. And, the Americans With Disabilities Act of 1990 ensures that reasonable workplace accommodations which compensate for functional limitations be determined and provided to individuals with identified cognitive disabilities such as NLD. Sample accommodations should be included in any diagnostic report.

Too often young adults forfeit their rights to accommodations because of fear of resistance or rejection. It is usually too late to approach a professor once a student has taken a test without accommodations and realizes that more time was needed. And, it may be too late to request job accommodations once dismissal proceedings have been initiated at the workplace. An employer is not responsible for accommodating disabilities which have not been disclosed to him or her. A young adult should get to know her professors or supervisors so that she can be comfortable voicing her needs.

4. Organizing Time and Place

Organization of time and place can pose a major problem for many individuals with NLD at the college level and in the workplace. Since she is unable to visualize or see the whole picture, this student will have difficulty setting realistic goals and priorities. She will tend to get overly bogged down by unimportant details. School or work situations can then overwhelm this individual and she will hit overload. Help her to seek a healthy balance of academic and social pursuits.

148   *The Source for Nonverbal Learning Disorders*

5. Help Foster Independence and Self-Determination

The course of this individual's life must be self-determined. Encourage a young adult to take part in as many opportunities for demonstrating her independence as are possible and plausible. Although parents must be strong advocates for a child with NLD during elementary, middle, and high school years, in college, and in the work world, a young adult will be expected to advocate on her own behalf. Parents should continue to provide guidance, support, encouragement and supervision. Hopefully, this child has been given the opportunity to develop skills in the areas of independent decision-making, problem solving, and the ability to express her own needs. Without these skills, the transition from high school to college or employment may be too overwhelming and ultimately defeating for the person with NLD.

Transition Strategies

1. The most significant problem an individual with NLD is likely to encounter in high school is resistance from teachers and peers. Educate both of these groups. Include provisions for staff inservice training in this student's IEP.

2. Leaving home is a major life change. As with any transition, approach it in increments. Gradually introduce practical life skills.

3. Before leaving high school, an individual's diagnosis should be confirmed or reaffirmed. There are distinct entitlements that go along with the diagnosis of NLD.

4. Organization of time and place can pose a major problem for many individuals with NLD at the college level and in the workplace. Since she is unable to visualize or see the whole picture, this student will have difficulty setting realistic goals and priorities. Help her to seek a healthy balance of academic and social pursuits.

5. The course of this individual's life must be self-determined. Encourage a young adult to take part in as many opportunities for demonstrating her independence as are possible and plausible.

Chapter 11
Adulthood and Independence

As public awareness and acceptance increase, the prognosis for adults with NLD can only improve . . .

Daniel, a tall, well-dressed man in his mid-forties, sat pensively through a lecture on NLD that I was giving, staring blankly up at me, with tears welling-up in his eyes. Afterward, as I was packing up my things, he cornered me and said, "I felt like you were holding up a mirror to me, describing everything that has happened in my life, and finally explaining to me why these things have happened to me, in terms I could actually understand. Could you please help me now?"

He was uncomfortably persistent, but all the same I was touched by Daniel's openness and honesty. We had never met before, yet he began telling me his life story right up to his present conflicts with his employer. Although my practice had previously been limited to consultation and educational therapy for children, I began working with Daniel immediately. I found him to be cooperative, talkative, and forthright.

Daniel was born and raised on the East Coast in a two-parent household with one older brother. His family was well-to-do and he attended private schools for most of his schooling. Daniel felt immense pressure from his parents to excel in school, especially since he wasn't athletically inclined, like his football player brother. At age 46, Daniel is a handsome, well-groomed, refined-looking gentleman. His general appearance is neat and precise, yet he remains a bachelor.

Throughout his schooling Daniel performed well academically, due in large part to his excellent verbal skills (reading and spelling). He reports that he had problems in the areas of gross and fine-motor coordination (he still can't hold a pencil properly), and relative difficulties with math. Daniel completed advanced-placement classes for English, History, and Latin in high school before continuing his education at a major university, where he received his B.S. in Business Administration.

Daniel's NLD wasn't diagnosed during his school years. However, school records support current evidence that he has always struggled with this condition. Early teacher comments include "works slowly," "doesn't follow instructions," "clumsy," and "talks too much." Since no diagnosis had been made, no type of intervention had previously been provided to Daniel regarding his NLD, and ADA disclosure was not provided to his employers regarding his NLD at the time of his employment.

Daniel relates that for most of his life he had depended exclusively upon his excellent memory skills to compensate for his areas of difficulty. Although things were always more difficult for him, he "managed to get by," as he put it. However, recently he had begun having some serious problems functioning at his job. Interventions in the workplace, which were utilized, and which failed to procure the desired results included the following:

- assistance from a technical consultant
- employer-imposed restrictive "performance program"
- requests for an "easier job" with the same employer
- an employer referral for neuropsychological testing for suspected "emotional interference with job performance"

Referring symptoms reported by Daniel to me included these:

- his inability to work under pressure (despite adequate training and intelligence)
- his misinterpretation of directives given to him by his employer
- he couldn't make sense of multi-dimensional computer screens
- he couldn't keep track of complicated orders
- he didn't "produce" enough to satisfy his employer
- he had difficulty finding his way around the large office building where he worked
- he was seen as inattentive by his employers (and subsequently, disciplinary actions and dismissal procedures had been initiated)

It was revealed that Daniel had switched jobs several times in the past, but had never actually been fired.

Daniel's office manager registered the following complaints in written critiques of Daniel and his job performance:

- "He requires constant supervision while on the job."
- "He requires a lot of one-on-one coaching and attention."
- "He can't remember a series of tasks."
- "He is often confused."
- "He fails to complete projects on time."
- "He frequently misinterprets instructions."

The neuropsychological assessment Daniel underwent revealed an 18-point discrepancy between his VIQ and PIQ. The examiner concluded, "[Daniel] appears to fit the description of an individual with nonverbal learning disabilities in many ways, in terms of history of learning and in terms of current test performance."

Several tell-tale traits stood out in my initial observations of Daniel. First, I couldn't help but notice that he evinced all the impressive

The Source for Nonverbal Learning Disorders

competencies that a person who is very verbal evokes in our society. It was obvious from our first session that Daniel relies heavily upon his verbal skills to mediate his difficulties. He displayed the passion of an attorney arguing a life or death case. Second, Daniel rarely, if ever, used the left side of his body. Daniel's left hand may as well have been paralyzed, as it lay limply in his lap throughout our interview. And third, it struck me that the difficulties he was having in the workplace, which Daniel so eloquently described to me, were no different from those that the children with NLD I've worked with endure throughout their schooling. The problems confronted in the workplace seem to be mere extensions of those encountered while in school. Apparently, NLD doesn't manifest differently in an adult.

NLD and Independence

Inquiries about the prognosis for success as an independent adult are among the most commonly asked questions I receive from parents of children with NLD. To date, there has only been one limited adult follow-up study tracking children with NLD into adulthood, so there is really no conclusive body of research information on the subject. And, when reviewing the findings of this particular study, the following must be kept in mind:

1. There were only eight individuals tracked.
2. All of these individuals were initially afflicted to the degree that they required clinical intervention during their childhood years.
3. The level of awareness regarding NLD and appropriate interventions and accommodations was limited at the time that these individuals were growing up.

Nonetheless, this study is alarming in that it found the subsequent outcome to be poor for all of the subjects involved. All had ongoing emotional and social problems. All were working in jobs below their level of intelligence and formal education. Some of these individuals were subsequently diagnosed with schizophrenia. Admittedly, this study does not present a reassuring image for parents. However, more studies are obviously needed before any sweeping conclusions can be drawn.

As public awareness and acceptance increase, the prognosis for NLD adults can only improve. Although all the NLD adults I have been acquainted with have, at some point in their lives, been treated for depression, most have had more satisfactory outcomes than the subjects of Rourke's 1986 study cited above. They are among the most tenacious adults I have ever met. Because life has always been a struggle for them, they don't ever expect anything to come easily for them.

A study of learning disabled children who went on to become highly successful adults found that a major factor contributing to their achievements in life was the fact that there had been someone in their childhood who understood and believed in them. This would seem to be all the more crucial for the child with NLD. Knowing that someone understands his circumstances and believes he has something worthwhile to contribute can supply the child with the support and encouragement he needs to navigate through the rough seas of childhood and adolescence.

Sarah's Story

Sarah is another NLD adult who consulted with me. She was a recent divorcée in her mid-forties when I first met her. Intelligent, attractive, and very outspoken, Sarah, at first glance, seemed to have a lot going for her. For a long time her difficulties had been masked by her own sense of determination and by a very domineering husband. Sarah had struggled throughout her schooling, knowing she was bright, yet wondering why "things came so much easier to everyone else." In her late-twenties, she finally received her undergraduate degree and, with school behind her, her future looked bright.

At that time, Sarah wanted to be a college lecturer in her field, but settled for a clerical position in a large company which promised rapid promotions. Within six months, Sarah was let go for poor reviews, citing her slow on-the-job performance and failure to meet deadlines. Sarah had been willing to put in a number of extra hours to complete her tasks, but her employer was unwilling to continue accommodating her after her initial break-in period. After a series of similarly unsuccessful vocational endeavors, Sarah married Kyle, she now says "almost as a stop-gap measure" to end her employment hassles. Although she was in her mid-thirties when she met Kyle, this was her first serious, long-term relationship. Shortly after their marriage, Sarah and Kyle had two daughters, Jolie and Luci, a year apart.

From the first day of her marriage, Sarah didn't attempt to work outside the home again. Her husband insisted that he be the breadwinner, and Sarah felt comfortable with her more predictable role as a housewife. She cared for her babies and tried to manage the house, but within a very short time, it seemed that she couldn't do anything well enough to please Kyle. He made fun of her because she couldn't hang a picture straight on the wall and because she had difficulty folding the washcloths into neat squares. Sarah couldn't locate items in her own home and she constantly got lost at the mall when she went out shopping. Often when she came out of the mall, she couldn't find her car. Once, she didn't even remember where she'd set down her baby.

154   *The Source for Nonverbal Learning Disorders*

Sarah's husband teased her and called her a poor parent. And Sarah believed him. "Why would he say that, if it weren't true?" she asked me years later, "after all, I did lose my own baby!" Shortly after the incident with the baby, Sarah began to feel overwhelmed by her responsibilities as a wife and mother. She thought things would improve when her girls started school because it was hard for her to concentrate with so many things going on in the house at the same time. For example, it was difficult for her to attend to her daughter's crying if she was right in the middle of fixing dinner. She didn't like to stop what she was doing and suddenly be forced to switch gears. Sarah insisted everything always be done in the same order every time; it was confusing to her when something was thrown at her out of sequence. She confided her anxieties to her doctor, who prescribed sedatives to her for "nervousness" and told her that she had "obsessive-compulsive tendencies."

Within the first five years of their marriage, Sarah's husband moved out of their bedroom and began sleeping on the living room couch. He spent more and more time away from home. On the weekends, he went skiing or hiking with his buddies. Kyle was very athletic and resented the fact that Sarah was such a klutz. But Sarah didn't mind staying home where she felt a certain degree of security. She always feared vacations and going to new places. Sarah even refused to accompany Jolie and Luci and her husband on a family trip to Disneyland because she was afraid she'd end up lost and confused.

And, it got to the point where Kyle rarely took Sarah out anymore, stating that she always said and did things that embarrassed him. He even accused her of "flirting" with his friends. But, if you had asked Sarah at that time, she would have told you "everything is fine" with her marriage, and that she and her husband just had "different interests." She says she "never saw it coming" when the sheriff arrived at her doorstep with divorce papers, after ten years of being married to Kyle.

Sarah's comments to me were, "He never *said* he didn't love me anymore," and "He never *told* me he wanted a divorce." Her husband insisted that "all the signs were there." He couldn't understand what difference it made whether he *told her* or *let her know* by his actions. His comments were, "We hadn't slept together for over five years. We never went out anymore. There was nothing remotely romantic about our existence. We were just two people sharing the same house and separately trying to raise our daughters. I avoided Sarah for years. It must have been obvious to her that our marriage was over. It was just a matter of how long we could keep up the charade." Even Sarah's attorney agreed, "All the signs were there, you must have been in denial . . . ."

But, Sarah wasn't "in denial." She never read the nonverbal cues her husband was communicating, no matter how obvious they were to any other observer. For her husband, their marriage dissolved when they "stopped doing things together as a couple." For Sarah, the day she received the divorce papers was her first indication that anything was wrong.

As part of the divorce process, Sarah was required by her husband's attorney to go through an employment evaluation and counseling. Because she showed signs of depression, she was also sent for a neuropsychological evaluation. The psychologist she was referred to noted, for the first time, that her past history and present symptomology were consistent with a nonverbal learning disorder. Looking back, Sarah finally had an explanation for all the difficulties she had encountered throughout her life. She was able to understand why everything always needed to be spelled out to her and why she so frequently got lost.

Sarah is now divorced and she and her daughters have moved back in with her parents. Her youngest daughter, eight-year-old Luci is showing some of the same coordination, visual-spatial-organizational, and social ineptitude problems that Sarah has struggled with all of her life. Although Luci is still in the process of assessment, Sarah has become a strong advocate for her daughter, seeking appropriate interventions for her at school. Sarah is also interested in starting support groups and other group activities for adults with NLD. A voracious reader, Sarah has read everything she can get her hands on regarding nonverbal learning disorders. She is a strong woman who has had to deal with the lack of awareness of her disorder by family, friends, and society at large for the better part of her life.

"Just knowing there's a reason for my problems," Sarah confided, "makes me feel my life will improve now. There have been so many times I thought I must be retarded — how could everyone else have such an easy time doing the very things that are such a struggle for me?"

The Individual with NLD Continues to Need Support In Adulthood

It is thought that adults with NLD often fail to maintain stellar employment records or satisfying marriages due to their "hidden" incompetencies. These misunderstood failures can lead to devastating emotional ramifications. It is imperative that individuals with NLD be trained for, and placed in, jobs which will not prove to be self-defeating, owing to their neuropsychological impairments. Even in adulthood, it is suggested by the Yale Child Study Center, these individuals must be provided "a certain degree of support and shelter." It is also preferable that their jobs do not involve "visual-motor skills and/or intensive social demands."

Owing to the "hidden" nature of nonverbal learning disorders, there is no immediate, outward appearance of the disability. ADA regulations apply on the job, but it is crucial to be able to identify the characteristics of this individual which might limit his or her success in an employment setting. It is these characteristics which will have the greatest impact upon this person's successful functioning in real life situations. What follows is a list of 14 specific behavioral characteristics common to individuals with NLD and appropriate CAMS to assist them in the workplace. *The individual with NLD is an intelligent, detail-oriented, highly motivated and dedicated employee*, but he or she also exhibits the following characteristics:

1. **Takes Longer to Complete an Activity**

   It often takes longer for an employee with NLD to complete an activity than her co-workers. This rules out assembly line and production type jobs. Slowness can irritate both supervisors and co-workers who work at a faster pace. Problems meeting deadlines may arise.

   Employers should be informed at the onset that the individual with NLD will need more time to complete tasks than other workers. One way to accommodate the individual with NLD is to allow her extra lead time. Giving this employee assignments in advance and allowing extra time for completion are standard strategies which can be utilized by an employer. Intense, high-pressure jobs aren't recommended for the individual with NLD.

2. **Has Difficulty Improvising or "Winging It"**

   The employee with NLD has difficulty "winging it" when expectations change. This means he won't compensate well in novel situations. Don't ask him to cover or fill in for coworkers with slightly different jobs. Make sure job responsibilities are clearly defined and don't alter day by day. The individual with NLD will have a difficult time working in a small businesses where he needs to be familiar with all aspects of the operation. Employers should learn to ask this individual to verbalize problems which arise. Step-by-step decision-making and problem-solving strategies will help bring novel situations into perspective.

3. **Has Difficulty Adjusting to Changes**

   Changes in routine, task sequence, personnel, working conditions, etc., are difficult for the employee with NLD. Always *preview* and *prepare* the worker for those changes. Post daily schedules in advance and discuss any changes in routine as soon as possible. Take time to thoroughly introduce and acquaint this individual with new staff members and new work areas.

4. Experiences Orientation and Visual-Spatial-Organizational Difficulties

The employee with NLD has visual-spatial-organizational difficulties. This causes disorientation to time and place, punctuality issues, and confusion when asked to complete several tasks simultaneously. This employee may constantly get lost in a large workplace. Stocking and delivery jobs aren't appropriate. Provide assignments which do not require driving.

Failure to complete assignments on the job may be the result of not knowing where to begin. Break large projects into small, easily assimilated tasks. (Remember, this worker doesn't visualize and will be overwhelmed by too much information given at once.) Don't assign numerous tasks simultaneously. More supervisory time may be needed, especially in the beginning. Provide appropriate CAMS, not reprimands.

5. Has Difficulty Generalizing Information

Difficulty in generalizing information will cause problems in jobs requiring discrimination of attributes or prediction of outcome from data. When presenting an assignment which requires the employee to generalize, follow these steps:

1. Review past information.
2. Present new findings/concepts/procedures.
3. Point out similarities, differences, and connections between the old and the new (these must be *verbally* pointed out, never assume . . .).
4. Indicate the current course of action which is appropriate given the generalizations which can be drawn.

6. Has Difficulty Following Diagrammatic Instructions

The individual with NLD shouldn't be asked to work from blueprints or diagrams. Remember, successive processing is a function of the left hemisphere, while simultaneous processing is a function of the right hemisphere. Diagrams, maps, drawings, symbolic figures, and designs all require the entire stimulus to be perceived at one time. Oral instructions, which are also written for clarification, are best. Present information to this worker successively, not simultaneously.

7. Shows Little Affect — Has a Blank Expression

The employee with NLD often has a blank expression on her face. This is problematic only in that it can have a negative impact on customers, coworkers, and supervisors. This individual may have difficulty in customer service positions working with the public because she can't read the facial expressions and body language of others, and because others are left puzzled (or offended) by her lack of facial expression or body language.

The Source for Nonverbal Learning Disorders

8. **Has Difficulty Following Multi-step Directions**
   Confusion over what to do and in what order it should be done can
   be at the core of an employee's failure to complete work assignments. Give instructions one step at a time. Tape record and/or
   write down multi-step instructions. Number and present the
   instructions in the most efficient sequence. Initially, pair this
   worker with a coworker who can help supervise and ensure that
   all the steps are completed.

9. **Asks Too Many Questions**
   Remember, the individual with NLD can't look and learn. He
   learns through verbal mediation. This can be aggravating to
   bosses and coworkers because they feel this individual isn't paying
   attention. This, in turn, creates problems in a group work environment. It is important to answer all of this employee's questions.
   The individual wants to learn and has an excellent memory for
   detail. If the employee's questions are taking up too much time at
   a staff meeting or during a presentation, arrange for another time
   when the employee's questions can be answered.

10. **Does Not Respond Appropriately to Nonverbal Cues**
    This can result in behavior which hinders production. The worker
    with NLD requires additional time for verbal reassurances, verbal
    directions, and verbal reminders. Avoid crowded work situations.
    Have this employee work in a small group, where her strengths
    will be accentuated and her weaknesses compensated for by the
    group. Avoid sarcasm. Say what you mean and mean what
    you say.

11. **Has Difficulty Performing Gross-motor Functions**
    Avoid occupations requiring manual labor (painter, carpenter),
    physical agility (landscape, mechanic), and/or the operation of
    heavy machinery. Ongoing balance problems exclude this indi-
    vidual from assignments which require working at various heights,
    on ladders or scaffolding, transporting equipment, etc.

12. **Has Difficulty Using Fingers in Fine-motor Tasks**
    Poor fine-motor dexterity limits this individual's ability to be a
    typist, a sewing machine operator, a TV repair person, etc. Avoid
    these categories of occupation.

13. **Will Process Information Slowly — Can't "Think Fast"**
    The individual with NLD is often slow to react. He should not
    work on production/assembly lines, around hazardous equipment,
    or at any position requiring quick reflexes (air traffic controller,
    fast food restaurant worker, police officer, etc.). Everyone at this

employee's workplace should be aware of the worker's need for extra time to respond.

14. Has Difficulty Copying Written Material

The individual with NLD shouldn't have a position which requires her to post information, copy written orders, do bookkeeping, or participate in inventory work. This employee should not be expected to copy information from an assignment board. At meetings requiring notes, ask a co-worker to use carbon paper or photocopy and share notes with this individual. Supervisors should provide written copies of any tasks which require transferring written information from one place to another.

160   *The Source for Nonverbal Learning Disorders*

Employment Characteristics

The individual with NLD is an intelligent, detail-oriented, highly-motivated, and dedicated employee, but may exhibit some of the following characteristics.

1. Takes Longer to Complete an Activity

2. Has Difficulty Improvising or "Winging It"

3. Has Difficulty Adjusting to Changes

4. Experiences Orientation and Visual-Spatial Difficulties

5. Has Difficulty Generalizing Information

6. Has Difficulty Following Diagrammatic Instructions

7. Shows Little Affect — Has a Blank Expression

8. Has Difficulty Following Multi-step Directions

9. Asks Too Many Questions

10. Does Not Respond Appropriately to Nonverbal Cues

11. Has Difficulty Performing Gross-motor Functions

12. Has Difficulty Using Fingers in Fine-motor Tasks

13. Processes Information Slowly — Can't "Think Fast"

14. Has Difficulty Copying Written Material

Chapter 12
NLD and Related Disorders

Presently, there isn't a formal medical diagnostic category for the syndrome of nonverbal learning disabilities . . .

Hyperlexia

Alex is a strong-willed five-year-old who has been reading nonstop since he was two years old. His mother noticed early on that although he was an insatiable reader, Alex didn't seem to comprehend the things he read. And, although he could talk, there were notable gaps in his language development. Alex also had behavioral problems that seemed to stem from not being able to pick up nonverbal cues from others. He threw major temper tantrums when his set routines were altered. Alex's mother pestered his pediatrician, who continually assured her "Don't worry, he's perfectly normal — every child develops at his own pace."

Finally, just prior to his registration for kindergarten, Alex's mother requested that the school district assess Alex's speech and language skills. A complete educational battery revealed that Alex's reading and spelling scores were exceptional for his age, whereas his language development was found to be significantly delayed. Echolalia, deficits in language pragmatics, and poor nonverbal communication skills were evidenced. Although a lot of his characteristics overlap with those of a child with nonverbal learning disabilities, Alex has excellent coordination. His diagnostic profile more accurately fits the standard diagnostic criteria for hyperlexia.

Asperger's Syndrome

Jaclyn is an eccentric little third grader with wild, frizzy curls and the all-knowing eyes of a very old soul. Small in stature and extremely verbal, she is intriguing to watch and fascinating to converse with. Jaclyn qualified for GATE (Gifted and Talented Education) this year, just prior to being referred for a special education assessment. Although she could read before starting school, Jaclyn currently experiences problems with written work, handwriting, and adaptive behavior in her mainstreamed classroom. Both her parents and her teachers have tried hard to understand this obviously gifted, but very unusual little girl.

My first interview with Jaclyn's mother stands out in my mind because she brought in the most complete and detailed baby book I have ever seen. Jaclyn was her first child and she meticulously recorded every aspect of Jaclyn's development. Her mother also had several portfolios of Jaclyn's "work," which consisted mainly of primitive drawings of sea otters, with long, rambling written narratives to accompany them. Her words dance all around the pages in a totally disorganized fashion. Jaclyn's grandparents had taken her to the Monterey Bay Aquarium when she was barely a year old and she has been obsessed with sea otters ever since, almost to the exclusion of any other interests. Jaclyn can tell you anything and everything about sea otters.

Jaclyn's mother reported that her developmental milestones were achieved within a normal time frame, except that she had a difficult time learning to walk (she took her first steps at 15 months, but didn't walk unaided until she was almost 2 years old). Because of her slight frame, she was easily transported in a stroller well past four years of age. When younger brother Nathaniel was born just before Jaclyn's fifth birthday, Jaclyn was told she needed to relinquish her stroller to him. But Jaclyn became hysterical and threw a temper tantrum every time the baby was placed in *her* stroller. It was never clear to Jaclyn's parents whether walking was actually difficult for Jaclyn or whether she just liked riding in her stroller, or exactly why it was so painful for her to give it up. Jaclyn was also still sleeping in her crib at almost five years of age, despite numerous efforts on her parents' part to get her to sleep in a regular bed. Clearly, Jaclyn didn't take well to any kind of change in her routine.

A few months after her brother was born, Jaclyn started kindergarten. During the first week of school, her teacher was already voicing concerns to Jaclyn's parents regarding Jaclyn's lack of adaptability at age five. Her mother agreed — Jaclyn always wanted things to stay the same. All new and different experiences were traumatic for Jaclyn. Her teacher also noted that, while at school, Jaclyn didn't interact with the other children, but stayed by herself most of the time. Jaclyn's favorite activity was drawing and coloring sea otters. Any topic of discussion in the class would elicit comments about sea otters from Jaclyn. Her teacher saw Jaclyn as lacking in maturity compared to the other children her age.

Jaclyn's parents continued to receive reports from school that their daughter was "eccentric" and "fussy." Jaclyn responded well to structured activities, but fell apart during unstructured free time. Any tasks involving reading were enjoyable, whereas hands-on projects annoyed her. Jaclyn's parents worked with her at home, but the reports from school didn't improve. By third grade, Jaclyn still had no close friends and was having so much difficulty completing assignments that her teacher referred her to the school's Student Study Team.

As expected, an assessment battery confirmed Jaclyn did extremely well on reading and spelling achievement tests, but had difficulty on tests of visual-motor integration and

DEFINITION

Asperger's syndrome (AS)
a severe developmental disorder characterized by major difficulties in social interaction and restricted and unusual patterns of interest and behavior.

fine-motor coordination. Although the overall results of her assessment battery were somewhat suggestive of a nonverbal learning disorder (including a PIQ significantly depressed in comparison to her VIQ), her restrictive, repetitive, and stereotypical patterns of behavior, coupled with an all-absorbing, narrow, and unusual area of interest (sea otters), led to the diagnosis of Asperger's syndrome.

Williams Syndrome

Another little girl whose behavior had perplexed her parents is six-year-old Maili. A sweet and sociable kindergartner with a broad, warm smile and "elfin" features, Maili now attends a special day class for developmentally-delayed children in her local SELPA (Special Education Local Planning Area). Her mother reports that Maili was a healthy, spunky infant. However, concerns about her first-born child began at six weeks of age, when Maili was first diagnosed with a heart murmur. At that time, her parents were assured that this was nothing to worry about. Her father, an insurance salesman, and her mother, a teacher's aide up until Maili's birth, had both decided it would be best if Maili's mother stayed home to care for their new baby.

As Maili grew, her mother's apprehensions grew. She wasn't really sure what she was so concerned about, though. Maili's checkups always produced reassurances that she was in good health. And, Maili was always in such a happy mood that she instantly charmed even total strangers. By 18 months of age, when Maili still hadn't shown any interest in walking, her parents began to question her pediatrician more insistently. He advised them to be patient. "Each child develops on her own schedule," he told them.

Sure enough, just before her second birthday, Maili took her first steps. And right about that time, she also uttered her first words. It wasn't long before she was asking pestering questions about everything. Once she started talking, her parents thought she would never stop! They breathed a sigh of relief, and thought, "Maybe Maili was just following her own schedule of development." They now look back upon that time of Maili's development as both exciting and frustrating. *Exciting* because things seemed to finally be falling into place for their daughter, and *frustrating* because they still had fears that their daughter wasn't developing at a normal pace.

Maili seemed to need extra protection when she was around other toddlers her age. She displayed a vulnerability that puzzled her parents, but everyone else dismissed their worries. "Stop babying her — she'll get into the swing of things," well-meaning friends and relatives advised. It was easy to feel overly protective towards Maili because she was quite small in stature. Her mother describes her as looking more like "a little stationary doll" than an active two-year-old. Repeated rounds to specialists only reinforced the notion that everything was normal with Maili. She had just been a slightly late bloomer.

However, when Maili turned three, on the advice of a teacher friend, Maili's mother had her evaluated by their local school district's early intervention team. Maili qualified for occupational therapy and speech and language services, to be provided by the school district. But, what was even more devastating to her parents was the pronouncement that Maili was mildly retarded. Testing showed that Maili was functioning at the level of an 18-month-old child — someone half her age.

DEFINITION

Williams Syndrome (WS)
a developmental disorder affecting connective tissue and the central nervous system. Characteristics of this disorder include heart disease, dysmorphic facial features, and poor visual-motor integration

Although their daughter had now been officially diagnosed as mildly retarded, her parents refused to believe that this label explained the whole story. The psychologist who administered the intelligence testing admitted to being puzzled by Maili's relative strengths in verbal skills as opposed to performance (nonverbal) skills (not the expected pattern for a child with delayed intellectual functioning).

Maili's long-term memory for information was outstanding. She remembered, verbatim, anything anyone ever told her. Maili's keen interest in the world baffled everyone. She repeated back news broadcasts and commercials, word for word. In fact, once she started talking, her verbal skills advanced at a rapid pace. Maili constantly asked questions about everything going on around her. Maili's father was already convinced that his daughter could not possibly be retarded when, at age five, Maili taught herself to read. Her interest and talent in musical pursuits also didn't conform with the typical profile he held of a retarded child.

Maili spent two years in an early intervention program before transferring to her SELPA's special day class for kindergarten, which she currently attends. She still can't catch a ball, balance on one foot, or tie her shoes. But, Maili can read far beyond the level of any of her classmates and she now plays the violin like a child prodigy. A visit to a pediatric cardiologist, as a follow-up for her heart murmur, led to the diagnosis of Williams Syndrome (a rare congenital disorder appearing in 1 out of every 20,000 individuals).

Many of the standard neuropsychological characteristics of a child with Williams Syndrome evidence considerable overlap with those of the child with NLD, including the following:

- verbal scores which exceed performance scores on intelligence testing (although usually not as markedly as in the case of a child diagnosed with NLD)

- good language skills and vocabulary (although often language is initially delayed, as was the case with Maili)

- poor gross and fine motor coordination

166 *The Source for Nonverbal Learning Disorders*

- problems with balance, poor visual-spatial perception
- relatively strong reading and phonics skills
- exceptional difficulty with handwriting and written language skills

In addition, a child with Williams Syndrome will often have specific musical aptitudes and experience mild to serious cardiovascular conditions. The IQ of a child with Williams Syndrome will range from *average* to *mild mental retardation*. In contrast, a child with NLD typically evinces average to very superior IQ. A child with Williams Syndrome usually has very distinctive, easily identifiable dysmorphic facial features; similar facial features are *not* found in children with NLD.

Another interesting distinction is the fact that a child with Williams Syndrome maintains an extremely friendly, gregarious personality throughout her life, whereas the child with NLD is usually only seen as highly sociable and outgoing during her early childhood years. As was discussed earlier, when the child with NLD approaches adolescence, she is extremely prone to developing internalizing disorders, such as depression and anxiety. Many clinicians believe this dissimilarity between the child with Williams Syndrome and the child with NLD results from the differing levels of intelligence within these populations. The brighter a child is to begin with, the more aware she is of her academic and social failures, and the more pressure she places upon herself to meet the expectations of those around her. A child with an IQ in the very superior range, therefore, would be much more likely to develop the various forms of internalizing psychopathology so often seen as secondary manifestations of NLD. Also, the child with Williams Syndrome almost always receives some type of early intervention, whereas, currently, the child with NLD is often left to struggle, flounder, and finally fail before receiving any help at school.

Link Between NLD and Williams Syndrome?

Are NLD and Williams Syndrome (WS) related disorders? This possibility is currently being explored by some researchers. Byron P. Rourke included a chapter on Williams Syndrome in his most recent (1995) book about nonverbal learning disabilities syndrome. Recently, I have begun including questions about heart conditions and musical abilities when obtaining histories from those clients of mine whose children have been diagnosed with NLD. Although this isn't a standard line of questioning, it is interesting to note that a large percentage of the children with NLD that I have had contact with do have a history of one or both of these variables. It is still too early to draw any specific conclusions, but this presents some interesting possibilities for future research. Ongoing genetic research suggests that Williams Syndrome is a contiguous gene disorder caused in part by the deletion of one copy of an elastin gene which has been isolated on chromosome #7 (7q11.23). Another effected gene is thought to play a role in developing spatial cognition, accounting for the visual-spatial abnormalities experienced by the child with Williams Syndrome.

An interesting facet of the research related to Williams Syndrome is that the researchers speak in terms of "partial" to "full" Williams syndrome. Full Williams syndrome appears to involve the deletion of at least nine genes located on the same region of chromosome #7. It is theorized that individuals with some, but not all, of the traits may be missing lesser amounts of DNA. An individual missing only one of these genes would just have the heart defect. Someone missing two of these genes might have the heart defect plus a spatial cognition problem. Three missing genes may mean heart problems, visual-spatial problems, and mental retardation, etc. Depending upon how many base pairs are deleted or shuffled, an individual could be left with partial to full Williams Syndrome. Defects in white matter development (in the right hemisphere of the brain) could be related to a missing gene which helps build body plans, including brain formation. When approached from this light, is it possible that NLD may be included in what genetic researchers refer to as "partial Williams Syndrome"?

Diagnoses Associated with NLD Symptoms

Presently, there isn't a formal medical diagnostic category for the syndrome of nonverbal learning disabilities. It isn't separately listed in the current DSM IV. A "Chinese menu" list style (pick two items from the first category, etc.) criteria hasn't been standardized to identify NLD. The official medical diagnosis your child receives will probably be one or a combination of the following:

- Developmental Disorder, Not Otherwise Specified (DD NOS)
- Learning Disability, Not Otherwise Specified (LD NOS)
- Cognitive Disorder, Not Otherwise Specified (CD NOS)

The child with NLD may also be saddled with a variety of other diagnostic labels, before the correct identification is finally made.

Severely Emotionally Disturbed is the most common misdiagnosis which school assessment teams, lacking in knowledge of NLD, come up with when assessing a child with NLD. NLD is *not* an emotional disturbance. Your child will probably *not* receive the correct educational services if he is incorrectly identified, so care must be taken in seeking professionals knowledgeable of NLD. Keeping this in mind, please note that there are also a number of diagnostic labels which convey the same meaning or which overlap to some degree with the syndrome of nonverbal learning disorders.

168 *The Source for Nonverbal Learning Disorders*

The terms *nonverbal learning disorder* or *nonverbal learning disability* and *right-hemisphere learning disability* are currently being used interchangeably. All denote a nonlanguage-based learning disability with deficits in motor skills, visual-spatial-organizational abilities, and social competencies. Other diagnostic classifications you may come across, which may be used to describe this learning disorder, or facets of it, include the following:

- learning disability, not otherwise specified
- developmental disorder, not otherwise specified
- cognitive disorder, not otherwise specified
- performance-based learning disability
- nondominant-hemisphere disorder
- right-hemisphere syndrome
- visual-motor learning disability
- developmental coordination disorder
- social perceptual disorder
- dyssemia

DEFINITION
dyssemia
difficulty in using and understanding nonverbal signs and signals; a nonverbal communication deficit

Hyperlexia (medical diagnosis is usually PDD NOS), Asperger's Syndrome (AS), and Williams Syndrome (WS) are currently diagnosed disorders which evidence some overlap with NLD. The chart on page 170 lists comparisons of NLD and other syndromes with social incompetencies.

As functional MRI's increase our knowledge of the intricacies of brain function, our understanding of NLD and other related nonlanguage-based disorders should also improve. This, in turn, should lead to the development of more and more effective intervention methods for these disorders. Meanwhile, it is up to parents and professionals to assume a protective and proactive role in accommodating the unique needs of these individuals.

We must advocate unceasingly to insure that the needs of these individuals are recognized and met in our schools, in our communities, and in the workplace. This is an urgent obligation we must all take on, and one which necessitates a significant investment of our time, energy, compassion and commitment, but one which is absolutely essential if we are to call ourselves a civilized society. Nonverbal Learning Disorders are, literally, killing our children. We can't be so callous as to sit back and watch this continue to occur, without doing everything we can to improve the situation!

Syndromes With Social Incompetencies

	Williams Syndrome (WS)	Autism	High Function Autism (HFA)	Pervasive Developmental Disorder (PDD)	Hyperlexia	Asperger's Syndrome (AS)	Nonverbal Learning Disabilities (NLD)
S P E E C H	delayed speech development — then very verbal — well-developed vocabularies	delayed	delayed	develops then regresses	delayed speech development, echolalia, abnormal prosody, early reading	no language delay — poor pragmatics and prosody	*early* speech and vocabulary development — poor pragmatics and prosody
I. Q.	retarded to low normal VIQ>PIQ	75% retarded PIQ>VIQ	normal; PIQ>VIQ	normal then regresses	normal; superior auditory and visual memory	normal to superior; VIQ>PIQ	normal to superior; VIQ>PIQ; verbal scores can be quite superior
M O T O R	significant gross, fine, and visual-motor problems; dysgraphia	gross motor = relative strength — fine motor problems	gross motor = relative strength, fine motor problems	coordination develops normally and remains good — may rarely regress	motor coordination usually superior — runs fast, climbs almost anything	clumsiness — gross motor is generally good, fine motor is poor	significant gross, fine, and visual-motor problems; dysgraphia
B E H A V I O R	outgoing/social, overly friendly, talkative, interest in music, sensitive to noise, obsessions	flapping, water play, toe walking, spinning, 10% savants, play impaired	disinterested, withdrawn, and aloof — may initiate inappropriate contact with others	restrictive, repetitive, and stereotypical patterns of behavior	obsessive-compulsive interest in certain topics; difficulty listening, complying with rules, and interacting with peers	"peculiar" — difficulties in social interaction, perseverating behaviors, restricted interests	lacking verbal communication skills (receptive and expressive) — naive and unable to "wing it"

 The Source for Nonverbal Learning Disorders

Glossary of Basic Terms

abstract thinking   the ability to think in terms of ideas

accommodations   adjustments or adaptations supplied to satisfy a need generated by an individual's disability

achievement test   a test of reading, mathematics, and/or language skills. The test provides scores based on grade-level equivalents. Each year the "average" child will gain one year's (1.0) growth on an achievement test.

alternate assessment   an evaluation using methods other than those applied to the majority of students in a class to assess a particular student's knowledge

anosognosia   the virtual inability to reflect on the nature and seriousness of one's own problems

Asperger's syndrome (AS)   a severe developmental disorder characterized by major difficulties in social interaction and restricted and unusual patterns of interest and behavior

assistive technology (AT)   under PL 92-142 (IDEA), schools are responsible for providing and maintaining computers and/or other assistive technology (AT) devices, and services, if such services are included in the student's IEP. Assistive technology, as expounded in PL 100-407, the Assistive Technology Act, for students with learning disabilities can include, but is not limited to, computers, taped-books, calculators, and electronic date books.

attention deficit disorder (ADD)   a neurologically-based condition in which the individual has difficulty directing or maintaining attention to everyday tasks such as learning and functioning

autism   a neurological condition characterized by severe language difficulties and a tendency to withdraw from external stimulation

Behavioral Intervention Plan (BIP)   a written plan for a child whose behavior significantly interferes with his learning and/or the other students' opportunity to learn, which specifically addresses those behaviors which interfere with learning. This plan must include a functional analysis of the child's behavior, as well as nonpunitive means for the child to acquire more acceptable replacement behaviors.

bilateral integration	the harmonious working relationship between the two sides of the body
body image	the mental representation an individual has of his own body, derived from internal sensation, postural changes, contact with outside objects and people, emotional experiences, and fantasies
CAMS	Compensations, Accommodations, Modifications, and Strategies
closure	coming up with a "whole" conclusion by assimilating all the "parts" of a concept or situation
compensations	counterbalancing variations; using an equivalent alternative means to work around areas of disability
comprehension	understanding
coordination	the unified action of muscle groups in performing complex movements
corpus callosum	wide band of neural fibers interconnecting the two cerebral hemispheres
crystallized intelligence	storehouse of general information/knowledge; overlearned skills; rote "old" learning; information based on past learning
deficit	a deficiency relating to a lack of skill or ability
development	the interaction between maturational processes and environmental influences
directionality	the projection of laterality (which has developed within oneself) to outside of oneself
discrimination	the ability to differentiate between two or more sensory stimuli
DSM IV	Diagnostic and Statistical Manual, fourth edition
dysgraphia	a specific disability in which handwriting is tremendously difficult
dyskinesia	an impairment of voluntary movement resulting in fragmented or incomplete movements; poor coordination
dyssemia	difficulty in using and understanding nonverbal signs and signals; a nonverbal communication deficit

   The Source for Nonverbal Learning Disorders

echolalia	repetition of exact words spoken by another person, used in place of original speech
etiology	source or origin of a syndrome or disease
eye-hand coordination	the integration of visual and tactile systems which enables the hand to be used as a tool of the visual processes
fine motor	the use of small muscle groups for specific tasks such as handwriting
finger agnosia	inability to interpret sensory impressions with fingers
fluid intelligence	practical, hands-on intelligence; how well a person "thinks on his or her feet"; how quickly and how competently a person processes and utilizes the information at his or her disposal
full inclusion	a placement in which a special education student receives instruction within the regular classroom setting for the entire school day
gestalt perception	deriving meaning from the "whole picture," without breaking it down into parts; "putting it all together"; a holistic view
hard signs	refer to unequivocal, medically documented signs of brain damage, such as brain surgery, cerebral bleeding, hemiplegia, brain tumor, or penetrating head injury (see also soft signs)
hyperlexia	a syndrome which interferes with speech, language, and social interaction. It may be accompanied by unusual or "different" behaviors. Children exhibit an intense fascination with letters, numbers, patterns, logos, etc., and a very precocious ability to read spell, write, and/or compute from as early as 18 months to before the age of five.
inclusive schooling	educating all children, with and without disabilities, together in heterogeneous classrooms. Materials are adapted, modified, and changed to accommodate the needs of individual students. Inclusive schooling allows disabled students to exercise their basic right to be educated in the same educational environment as their peers.
Individualized Education Program (IEP)	the specific educational plan and strategies designed for a student who qualifies for special education services under PL 92-142 (IDEA). The IEP contains written annual goals and short-term instructional objectives tailored for the individual student, as well as standards by which these goals will be

accomplished. Modifications and accommodations needed by the child in order to be successful in an inclusive setting are documented in her IEP. Good IEPs are always driven by the child's needs. They define the kinds of support the child will need and list the services the school staff will need to provide in order for these goals to be achieved.

Individualized Transition Program (ITP) — the specific transition plan and strategies required for a student who is 16 years of age or older, who qualifies for special education services under PL 92-142 (IDEA). The ITP contains a plan for the successful transition of the student from school to work, additional training or higher education, and community living.

impairment — a neurological blockage or barrier to expected development

integration — see full inclusion

intervention — the therapeutic and/or educational methods employed to aid a child once a disability has been diagnosed

Intervention-Based Multifactored Evaluation — a collaborative, problem-solving process which focuses upon concerns which affect the learner's educational progress within a learning environment

kinesthesis — the sensory knowledge and awareness of the body and body parts in space; includes awareness of balance and motion

laterality — the internal awareness an individual has of the two sides of his body

least restrictive environment — a term from PL 92-142 (IDEA) requiring that, to the greatest extent possible, students with disabilities must be educated with their non-disabled peers

left hemisphere — the area of the brain which is specialized for processing verbal or language-based information. This includes the rote memory, linguistic, symbolic, linear, and analytical functions of an individual.

low incidence disability — a severely disabling condition with an expected incidence rate of less than one percent of the total statewide enrollment for kindergarten through grade twelve

mainstreaming — placing students with special needs in regular classroom settings with support services

midline	the imaginary line from the tip of the head to the feet, which separates the body into halves
modality	a sensory mode utilized by an individual to receive and/or acquire information (i.e. auditory, visual, tactile, kinesthetic)
modifications	adaptations made in curriculum, presentation method, or the environment to provide support for the individual student
nonverbal learning disorders (NLD)	a neurological condition believed to result from damage to the white matter connections in the right-hemisphere, which are important for intermodal integration. Three major categories of dysfunction present themselves:

1. motoric (lack of coordination, severe balance problems, and difficulties with fine graphomotor skills)
2. visual-spatial-organizational (lack of image, poor visual recall, faulty spatial perceptions, and difficulties with spatial relations)
3. social (lack of ability to comprehend nonverbal communication, difficulties adjusting to transitions and novel situations, and deficits in social judgment and social interaction).

occupational therapy	activity intended to promote specific physical and/or sensory skills a child lacks
parallel activity	an alternate assignment given to a student, in which the outcome achieves the same goal, but the methods and materials used to reach that outcome may be different
perception	the mental interpretation of sensations receives from stimuli
perceptual-motor	the functioning of the perceptual and motor processes together
perseveration	the continued repetition of words or motions after the point where they no longer serve a useful purpose
pragmatics	the relation between signs or linguistic expressions and their users
previewing	presenting the student with materials to familiarize him with the subject matter before class instruction or a test
prosody	the variations of emphasis and intonation in speech
psycho-motor	the relationship between the brain and the muscles

right hemisphere	the area of the brain which is specialized for processing non-verbal or performance-based information. This includes the visual-spatial, intuitive, organizational, evaluative, and gestalt (holistic) processing functions of an individual.
sensory integration	the brain's ability to take in and synthesize multi-modality experiences perceived by the senses (vision, hearing, smell, taste, touch, motion, and temperature)
Sensory Integrative Therapy (SIT)	developed by Dr. Jean Ayres, an occupational therapy treatment program consisting of exercises which encourage the individual to use as many nerve-cell connections as possible
sensory-motor	the relationship between sensation and movement
social imperception	difficulty interpreting social situations; inability to read facial expressions, tone of voice, body language, or other cues
soft signs	refer to minimal behavioral deviations in a child, reported by a neurologist, where traditional neurological examination shows no hard signs of brain damage or dysfunction. These indications, such as neuromuscular clumsiness, involuntary twitching movements in the hands, and poor directional sense, are strongly suggestive of abnormal functioning of the central nervous system.
speech and language therapy	treatment of speech and language disorders, not limited to articulation problems, and including pragmatic language
strategies	careful plans or methods employed towards a goal
support services	speech and language therapy, occupational therapy, adaptive physical education, etc.
supportive teaching	making accommodations and modifications which allow a special education student to experience success in a regular classroom
syndrome	a set of symptoms occurring together
tactile	having to do with touch
tactile-kinesthetic	relating to the sense of touch and the feeling of movement; touching and doing

The Source for Nonverbal Learning Disorders

visual discrimination	visual adeptness at perceiving likenesses and differences in geometrical figures, symbols, pictures, and words
visualization	the ability to picture, relate, and manipulate visions within one's mind
visual-motor	the relationship between visual input and motoric output, as in copying text
visual-motor integration	the coordination of visual information with motor processes
visual-perception	how an individual interprets the things he sees
visual-spatial	the spatial configuration of the things one sees
Williams Syndrome (WS)	a developmental disorder affecting connective tissue and the central nervous system. Characteristics of this disorder include heart disease, dysmorphic facial features, and poor visual-motor integration.
WISC-III	Wechsler Intelligence Scale for Children (third edition). Five subtests make up the verbal scale, and five subtests make up the performance scale. The WISC-III provides three IQs: verbal, performance, and full-scale.
white matter	long myelinated fibers in the brain
504 Plan	Section 504 of PL 93-112 (the Rehabilitation Act of 1973) defines a disabled individual as anyone who experiences a "mental, psychological, or physiologic disorder which interferes with [that] individual's civil right to one or more major life activities." If a student has a disabling condition which interferes with his ability to learn or perform up to his ability in school, the school district must draw up a plan of appropriate CAMS to be implemented for this student. All special education students covered under PL 92-142 (IDEA) are automatically covered under Section 504 of PL 93-112. An IEP can serve in place of a 504 plan.

Support and Resources

Professional Intervention and Training:

An NLD Hotline devoted to helping those individuals struggling with NLD has been established to answer questions and match parents' needs with a qualified professional. If you are interested in NLD workshops, staff inservice training, and/or presentations by Sue Thompson or others, please call 831-624-3542.

A graduate-level course, *Understanding, Identifying, and Servicing the Child with Nonverbal Learning Disorders for Educators*, is being offered through the University of California Extension, Santa Cruz, Education Department. For dates and times of upcoming courses, call 831-748-7385.

Parent organizations:

Parents of children with low-incidence disabilities like NLD can benefit from exchanging ideas and discussing their problems with each other. It is also helpful to attend lectures, workshops and conferences which can help you to better understand your child's strengths and limitations.

Asperger's Syndrome Education Network of America (ASPEN) is a newly-formed non-profit organization dedicated to helping families and individuals with AS and related disorders and those professionals who work with them. Their goals are to help interested parents set up local support groups for families and adults; to advocate for medical and legal issues; to educate parents, professionals, and the community about AS and related disorders; to sponsor workshops, and to maintain a web site (Online Asperger's Syndrome Info & Support — O.A.S.I.S.). They will have a newsletter, also. for membership information, contact:

> Rhona Silver
> 7412 Stonehurst Rd. S.
> Jacksonville FL 32277-3755
> http://www.udel.edu/bkirby/asperger/

Learning Disabilities Association of America (LDA) is a non-profit, volunteer organization whose purpose is to advance the education and general welfare of children of normal or potentially normal intelligence who have learning disabilities of a perceptual, conceptual, or coordinative nature. There are over 600 chapters located throughout the United States. LDA publishes six editions of *Newsbriefs*, per year. For membership information contact:

> Mrs. Jean Peterson, Executive Director
> Learning Disabilities Association of America
> 4156 Library Road
> Pittsburgh PA 15234
> (412) 341-1515 or (412) 341-8077
> Fax: (412) 344-0224
> http://www.ldanatl.org

 The Source for Nonverbal Learning Disorders

Learning Disabilities Association of California (LDA-CA), the California chapter of the Learning Disabilities Association of America, is a non-profit volunteer organization of parents and professionals whose purpose is to promote and support the education and general welfare of learning disabled children and adults of potentially normal, or superior intelligence who manifest learning, perceptual and/or behavioral disabilities. They publish four editions of *The Gram*, per year. Excerpts from this book appeared in a series of articles published in *The Gram*. For membership information contact:

> LDA-CA State Office
> 655 Lewelling Blvd., #355
> San Leandro CA 94579
> (415) 343-1411
> Fax: (415) 343-1854

East Bay Learning Disabilities Association (East Bay-LDA), the Alameda and Contra Costa County affiliate of the Learning Disabilities Association of America and Learning Disabilities Association of California, is a non-profit organization of parents and professionals dedicated to the improvement of education and life for individuals of average to superior intelligence with learning, perceptual, and/or behavioral challenges which are associated with dysfunctions of the central nervous system. Their local newsletter is published four times each year. For membership information contact:

> East Bay-LDA
> P.O. Box 5513
> Berkley, CA 94705
> (510) 433-7934

SHARE Support, Inc. is a non-profit, parent-based organization which offers support and education to parents, professionals, and educators working with children with learning, behavioral, and/or physical differences. Their local newsletter, the *Support Report*, is published four times each year. SHARE Support, Inc., held its first annual Nonverbal Learning Disorders Symposium in April of 1997, and they are currently co-sponsoring a survey of individuals with NLD with Children's Hospital in Oakland. To learn more about future NLD symposiums, the NLD survey, or membership information, contact:

> SHARE Support, Inc.
> P.O. Box 2379
> Danville CA 94526
> (510) 820-4079

> Note: Audiotapes from the SHARE Support NLD Symposium
> are available from:
> Contemporary Medical Education
> 913 San Ramon Valley Blvd., Suite 288
> Danville CA 94526
> 1-800-920-3655
> http://www.contemp-med-ed.com

Web Sites & Bulletin Boards (Support On-Line):

America Online subscribers can access the NLD bulletin board in this manner: Click on "Families" in the channel menu, then select "Education," "Special Education." Then click on "Message Boards" and scroll to the "Nonverbal Learning Disorders 2" folder.

LD Online is a place to learn, find help, and exchange ideas:
http://www.ldonline.org/

C.H.A.D.D. contains the latest A.D.D. information:
http://www.chadd.org/

American Hyperlexia Association maintains a site for material on hyperlexia:
http://www.hyperlexia.org/

EdLaw provides information on special ed. law:
http://www.access.digex.net/~edlawinc/

Online Asperger's Syndrome Information and Support (O.A.S.I.S.):
http://www.udel.edu/bkirby/asperger

The NLD Line — this site is forthcoming and a web address is unavailable at this time. You will, however, be able to link to it from the O.A.S.I.S. site listed above.

Parent's Educational Resources Center — PERC was founded in 1989 by Charles and Helen Schwab Foundation as a community service to improve the lives of families with learning disorders:
http://www.perc-schwabfdn.org/

Parents Helping Parents — PHP is a parent support organization:
http://www.php.com/

180 *The Source for Nonverbal Learning Disorders*

References

Bauer, Stephen, MD, MPH. "Asperger Syndrome." *The Gram.* 30.1 (1996): 11-15.

Bigler, Erin D. "On the Neuropsychology of Suicide." *Journal of Learning Disabilities* 22.3 (1989): 180-185.

Bursuck, William. "A Comparison of Students with Learning Disabilities." *Journal of Learning Disabilities* 22.3 (1989): 188-194.

Brumback, R.A. "Nonverbal Learning Disabilities, Aspergers Syndrome, Pervasive Developmental Disorder — Should We Care?" *Journal of Child Neurology.* 11 (1996): 427-429

Fletcher, Jack M. "Nonverbal Learning Disabilities and Suicide: Classification Leads to Prevention." *Journal of Learning Disabilities,* March 1989: 176-179.

Foss, Jean. "Nonverbal Learning Disabilities and Remedial Interventions." *Annals of Dyslexia*, Vol. XXXXI 1991: 128-140.

Gaddes, William H., and Dorothy Edgell. *Learning Disabilities and Brain Function.* New York: Springer-Verlag, 1994.

Hynd, G.W., et al. "Brain Morphology in Developmental Dyslexia and Attention Deficit Disorder/Hyperactivity." *Archives of Neurology*, Vol. 47. 1990: 919-926.

Kagan, J., et al. "Information Processing in the Child: Significance of Analytic and Reflective Attitudes." *Psychological Monographs*, Vol. 78. January :578.

Klin, A., et al. "Validity and Neuropsychological Characterization of Aspergers Syndrom: Convergence with Nonverbal Learning Disabilities Syndrome." *Journal of Child Psychology and Psychiatry*, Vol 36.7 (1995):1127-1140.

Kowalchuk, Brian, and John D. King. "Adult Suicide Versus Coping w. Nonverbal Learning Disorder." *Journal of Learning Disabilities,* 22.3 (1989): 177-179.

Levine, Melvin D., M.D. *Developmental Variation and Learning Disorders.* Cambridge, Mass.: Educators Publishing Service, Inc., 1987.

Levine, Melvin D. *Educational Care.* Cambridge, Mass.: Educators Publishing Service, Inc., 1997.

Little, Sara S. "Nonverbal Learning Disabilities and Socioemotional Functioning: A Review of Recent Lit." *Journal of Learning Disabilities.* Dec. 1993: 653-665.

Mehrabian, A. and S.R. Ferris. "Inference of Attitudes from Nonverbal Communication in Two Channels." *Journal of Consulting Psychology*, Vol. 31. 1967: 248.

Mesulam, M.M. and S. Weintraub. "Developmental Learning Disabilities of the Right Hemisphere." *Archives of Neurology*, Vol. 40. 1983: 463-468.

Myklebust, Helmer R. "Nonverbal Learning Disabilities: Assessment and Intervention." *Progress in Learning Disabilities,* 3 (1975): 85-121.

Nowicki, Stephen, Jr., Ph.D., and Marshall Duke, Ph.D. *Helping the Child Who Doesn't Fit In*. Atlanta: Peachtree Publishers, Ltd., 1992.

Nowicki, Stephen, Jr., Ph.D., and Marshall Duke, Ph.D. *Teaching Your Child the Language of Social Success*. Atlanta: Peachtree Publishers, Ltd., 1996.

Older, F., M.D. "Patients Who Say Little: A Syndrome of Nondominant- Hemisphere Deficit." *Psychiatric Times,* 16 January 1994.

Pennington, B.F. *Diagnosing Learning Disorders: A Neuropsychological Framework*. New York: Guilford Press, 1991.

Rosen, Warren D. *Nonverbal Learning Disabilities: Socioemotional and Pragmatic Quagmires* (lecture on tape). Chicago, IL: Association of Educational Therapists, April 27, 1996.

Rourke, Byron P. "Nonverbal Learning Disabilities & Socioemotional Disturbance." *Journal of Learning Disabilities,* 22.3 (1989): 186-187.

Rourke, Byron P. *Syndrome of Nonverbal Learning Disabilities: Neurodevelopmental Manifestations*. New York: Guilford Press, 1995.

Rourke, Byron P., et. al. "A Childhood Learning Disability that Predisposes Those Afflicted to Adolescent and Adult Depression and Suicide Risk." *Journal of Learning Disabilities*, Vol. 22. March 1989: 169-175.

Rourke, Byron P., M.D. *Nonverbal Learning Disabilities: The Syndrome and the Model*. New York: Guilford Press, 1989.

Thompson, Sue. "Nonverbal Learning Disorders: Part 1 — An Introduction and Part 2 — Identifying Nonverbal Learning Disorders." *The Gram*. 30.3 (1996):7-10 & "Nonverbal Learning Disorders: Part 3 — Servicing Nonverbal Learning Disorders." *The Gram*. 30.4 (1996):7-10.

182 *The Source for Nonverbal Learning Disorders*